The Entrepreneur in Youth

NEW HORIZONS IN ENTREPRENEURSHIP

Series Editor: Scott Shane
SBC Professor of Economics, Weatherhead School
of Management, Case Western Reserve University, USA

This important series is designed to make a significant contribution to the development of Entrepreneurship Studies. As this field has expanded dramatically in recent years, the series will provide an invaluable forum for the publication of high-quality works of scholarship and show the diversity of issues and practices around the world.

The main emphasis of the series is on the development and application of new and original ideas in Entrepreneurship. Global in its approach, it includes some of the best theoretical and empirical work with contributions to fundamental principles, rigorous evaluations of existing concepts and competing theories, historical surveys and future visions. Titles include original monographs, edited collections, and texts.

Titles in the series include:

The Entrepreneur in Youth

An Untapped Resource for Economic Growth, Social Entrepreneurship, and Education

Marilyn L. Kourilsky

Professor and Director, Institute for the Study of Educational Entrepreneurship, University of California at Los Angeles (UCLA), USA

William B. Walstad

Professor of Economics, University of Nebraska-Lincoln, USA

with Andrew Thomas

Postdoctoral Fellow, University of California at Los Angeles (UCLA), USA

NEW HORIZONS IN ENTREPRENEURSHIP

Edward Elgar
Cheltenham, UK • Northampton, MA, USA

Published by
Edward Elgar Publishing Limited
Glensanda House
Montpellier Parade
Cheltenham
Glos GL50 1UA
UK

Edward Elgar Publishing, Inc.
William Pratt House
9 Dewey Court
Northampton
Massachusetts 01060
USA

A catalogue record for this book
is available from the British Library

ISBN 978 1 84542 250 9

Printed and bound in Great Britain by MPG Books Ltd, Bodmin, Cornwall

Contents

Tables

Foreword

Starting a business and giving birth have features in common. They are both wonderful, exhilarating, ultimately rewarding, and – as any woman who has given birth and started her own business can attest – indisputably painful! But just as medical science and natural, holistic childbirth practices have improved the experience of having and raising children, this book by Drs. Kourilsky and Walstad seeks to improve the experience of young people who want to give "birth" to and "raise" their own for-profit and non-profit enterprises.

The importance of the research reported in this book cannot be overemphasized. The authors found, in their nationwide investigation of high school students' attitudes toward and knowledge of entrepreneurship that a majority of these young people would like to start businesses of their own. What is the major reason for their interest? They want to be their own bosses and achieve their full potential. Already, at their young ages, they understand how working for others may limit their accomplishments. They want to stretch their wings and show the world what they can do. We also learn from the authors that young people are aware of their own educational shortcomings. They want to learn about entrepreneurship and business management.

But most exciting for me was the revelation that young people in the United States today feel strongly that business owners are under an obligation to contribute to their communities in ways that go beyond merely creating jobs and paying taxes. What is more, a majority of young people surveyed aspires to start non-profit or charitable organizations of their own. What an important finding! For young people in the United States today, it is no longer an either/or proposition: should they make money, or should they help others? These young people seem to intuit on some level that they can do both. This belief is one that I have, of course, long shared. When I started Mrs. Gooch's Natural Foods Markets, I had the strong conviction that good living could also be good business and vice versa. This was an unusual concept for many customers and business people in the late seventies, but today it seems to enjoy much greater currency, and I hope this change in attitude is a legacy for which I can take some small credit.

The authors, in writing this book, have motivations that are similar to mine. Just as I wanted to improve how people ate and shopped for food, these scholars want to improve how young people learn about and prepare for a lifetime of achievement. The authors know whereof they speak. Marilyn Kourilsky and William Walstad are world-renowned, leading experts on entrepreneurship and economic education.

These educators' book tells us what we need to do. First, it is clear we should listen to what young people say they want. They want their schools to be more nourishing places. Of course, I am interested in natural, nourishing foods and wellness practices, but the principle extends to nourishing dreams. The authors of this book point out tellingly that schools too often encourage – either indirectly or more directly – a consumerist mindset. It is not that schools dish up instructional "junk food"; it is just that the "content areas" and "assessment criteria" in today's focused and efficient curricula are highly processed. Sometimes your health is affected as much by what you do not eat as what you do. Too often, educational product is analogous to refined white flour – it has the kernel of the original grain, but misses the healthful germ and fiber. One might say it is predigested! Why not ask students themselves to recognize raw opportunities of entrepreneurship and "process" them into enriched business plans? Along the way, they will acquire the entrepreneurial thinking and economic skills they have requested. This book provides evidence that young people have an appetite for this kind of education.

Giving birth is a blessing, but children are also our offerings to future generations; we send them forth and hope that we have prepared them to do great things and to contribute to making the world a little bit better. This book shows that, as a society, we have been doing an adequate job. Our children want to start their own enterprises that will prosper and provide good jobs for people in their communities and worthwhile experiences for their employees and customers. Many of them also aspire to build non-profit or charitable organizations whose major goals are to improve life on our planet. We have raised our children with the right values. It is now our obligation to ensure they are prepared to accomplish their aspirations. This book assures me our best economics and entrepreneurship educators and educational researchers know what needs to be done. As Founder of Mrs. Gooch's Natural Foods Markets and subsequently Sandy Gooch Enterprises, I have been privileged to pursue socially beneficial initiatives through the entrepreneurial process and have been recognized nationally and internationally with awards and distinctions such as being selected as one of The Leading Women Entrepreneurs of the World™ for 2001. I was the only woman to be chosen among the "Fifty Visionary Leaders Who Transformed Food Retailing" by Supermarket News, and one of the "Top 50 Women Business Owners" in the United States recognized by the National Foundation of Women Business Owners (NFWBO). This seminal book reveals through the voices of our youth their desire for education that may lead to similar opportunities for enacting social change and achieving meaningful recognition. It is now up to the policymakers, administrators and teachers who read this book to take the necessary steps toward the laudable goal of giving every child access to the skills and knowledge necessary for them to achieve their entrepreneurial dreams.

Sandy Gooch

Acknowledgments

The goal of this book is to produce a comprehensive assessment of high school student knowledge, opinions, and education with respect to entrepreneurship in both the for-profit and not-for-profit sectors. The data and findings reported in the book are derived from a series of national surveys conducted with high school students, members of the general public, and owners of small businesses during an eight-year span bridging the transition to the twenty-first century.

The book is organized around three major themes. The first theme investigates the strong interest of high school youth in becoming entrepreneurs in both the for-profit and not-for-profit sectors. It examines the depth of this interest and how it can be encouraged through appropriate entrepreneurship education. The second theme explores the multiple factors that contribute both to for-profit and to social entrepreneurship among youth by focusing on knowledge, personal characteristics, and attitudes. It explores youth's views and understanding of the often surprising and neglected relationship between entrepreneurship and philanthropy, and the demonstrably significant capacity for social entrepreneurship to benefit the local community. The third theme offers perspectives on the thinking and opinions of high school students using longitudinal comparisons and also comparisons with the general public and small business owners. Throughout the book, special attention is given to the influence of gender, race, and ethnicity on perceptions and understanding of entrepreneurship among youth.

Our book would not have been possible without the help we received from other organizations. The authors would like especially to acknowledge the John Templeton Foundation for its encouragement, patience, and its financial support in bringing this book project to fruition. We also thank the Ewing Marion Kauffman Foundation for its sponsorship of the national surveys on entrepreneurship that were administered to various groups over the years and the access to the data that we used for analysis and reporting in this book.

We also benefited from the advice we received from senior consultants at The Gallup Organization in final preparation of the surveys that we wrote and also from their work on the sampling, survey administration, and data processing. In this regard, we appreciated the time given by the thousands of survey respondents from across the country that consisted of high school students, members of the general public, and owners of small businesses, who were willing to donate their valuable time to answer the questions on our survey rather than hanging up when they heard an unfamiliar voice on the other end of the line.

The writing of this book took more time than we ever anticipated, in part because of the volume of the data we had to study, and also because we could never quite find all the time we wanted to give to this project given our responsibilities at UCLA and Nebraska. We were helped along in the process by the work of Andrew Thomas, who discussed ideas for the book, prepared content for our review, and found references and resources to advance the project.

We also greatly appreciated the understanding of Alan Sturmer at Edward Elgar, who encouraged our work from the beginning to end. Sharon Nemeth at the University of Nebraska-Lincoln devoted many countless hours to preparing the manuscript in its final form and did a superb job of typing and revising the text, formatting the tables and the page layouts, and proofreading the contents. On a personal note, we must recognize the strong endorsements and good support and feedback we received from Greg Kourilsky and Tammie Fischer as we worked through the different parts of the project over the past three years.

This book should offer new insights about youth entrepreneurship that have the potential to expand more economic growth and innovation in the economy, promote more social entrepreneurship and philanthropy, and give youth a better education that prepares them to be more entrepreneurial in their actions and careers. Of course, no academic work of this sort is ever finished because there are other ideas to consider, other connections that could be made, or pieces that could be added. We want this book to stimulate such thinking in the reader.

Marilyn L. Kourilsky

William B. Walstad

1. Finding the Entrepreneur in Youth

Entrepreneurial spirit, in its broadest sense, is a vital ingredient in the achievements of every person who succeeds beyond his or her original means. The person who starts a small business has something in common with the sales worker who suggests a better procedure for appealing to customers, the engineer who develops a new technique for improving quality control in a manufacturing system, the doctor or lawyer who opens his or her own practice, the real estate agent who finds new ways to market houses, a political activist whose actions induce a change in the law, and an academic who starts a research center. They all show, to a greater or lesser degree, the entrepreneurial spirit that drives them to create new processes, new products, or new ventures from the challenges and opportunity they see and experience.

Somewhere along the path to success in most careers, individuals encounter the need for entrepreneurial acumen. Some of these individuals may have learned this acumen through life or work experiences, however idiosyncratic and incomplete such learning may be over a lifetime. Other individuals may have been fortunate enough to have attended a college or university, and perhaps while at such institutions, they may have gained some entrepreneurial knowledge, skills, and habits of mind. What is especially unlikely is that this type of education ever gets provided to individuals in the prime of their secondary education when they are especially receptive to entrepreneurship. When high school students ask how they can succeed in their careers, they receive an education that largely omits preparation for entrepreneurship and the development of their entrepreneurial thinking.

This book's central thesis is that there is an entrepreneur in youth who, if given a quality education, can be nurtured and stimulated. If such an education for entrepreneurship was provided in high schools, it would have a lifelong effect on students' thinking and actions, and significantly contribute to their career success as adults, regardless of whether they ever launch an enterprise. Entrepreneurship education for youth also would make lasting contributions to social mobility, communities, and economic growth.

1

LISTENING TO THE VOICES OF YOUTH

To say so many successful people use entrepreneurial skills to achieve success is admittedly to use an expansive definition of "entrepreneurial." The term *entrepreneur* is derived from the French verb *entreprendre,* which literally means "to take from between," and suggests the role of bridging two entities: perhaps a buyer and a seller, a person who needs something and a person who can meet that need.[1] Typically, an entrepreneur is an individual who satisfies an unmet market demand in a particular area. The point that needs to be made at the start of this book, however, is that the thought processes and skills employed by such an individual are capabilities that can be generalized to all kinds of endeavors. Most important, they include the ability to recognize opportunity that others have overlooked and the propensity to act on that opportunity where others may hesitate. To be able to do this, individuals must be encouraged to frame problems as "disguised opportunities." It is a process that can be called "entrepreneurial thinking," or having an "entrepreneurial mindset."

For example, the disguised opportunity that 13-year-old Kenya James recognized was that none of the magazines on the market were targeted at girls like her – young African Americans. As a consequence, she founded *Blackgirl Magazine,* a periodical that not only entertained, but also empowered young African American females.[2] The goal of her magazine was to promote positive messages and imagery, while offering insightful coverage of history, culture, lifestyle, and entertainment.

What this teenager and others like her have in common is that they have learned to view problems, such as a gap in the teenage magazine market – as "demands" for solutions. These entrepreneurial teenagers noticed people's complaints, inconveniences, difficulties, and assorted problems and took action to make a positive difference in trying to solve them, for their own benefit and the benefit of others. They have an entrepreneurial mindset in what they have chosen to do and be.

The knowledge and skills associated with being able to *act* on opportunity once it is recognized include, but are not limited to, finance, budgeting, marketing, managing people, and economics, together with an understanding of the role of government in taxing and regulating ventures. Kenya realized that her biggest obstacle to starting a business was lack of financing. She was able to realize her dream by baking and selling cakes until she socked away $1500. This amount of money, however, was insufficient to put out the first issue of her magazine, so she pre-sold print advertising at a discounted price to businesses that she and her friends frequented. This combination of seed money and the advanced sales of advertising allowed the magazine to launch.

The pages of this book could be filled with examples of young people who through some form of mentoring or education gained the confidence and know-how to act on their opportunities and to initiate their own ventures, both for-profit and non-profit.[3] Providing such examples, however, is not the purpose of this book. Just as some athletes are not "born athletes," but achieve their success through interest, practice and persistence, not all entrepreneurs or entrepreneurial thinkers emerge when they are young with an entrepreneurial mindset and a full set of capabilities. Coaching immensely benefits both "natural" athletes, for whom success comes easily, and other athletic participants who must work harder to succeed.

Similarly, a high-level program of entrepreneurship education would benefit all high school students. It would accelerate the entrepreneurial thinking and behaviors of those youth who are naturally inclined and skilled in the ways of thinking and acting as entrepreneurs. It also would develop and expand the entrepreneurial knowledge and skills in those youth who have not yet recognized the many advantages that entrepreneurial know-how offers for creating opportunities and achieving long-term goals. Even for those high school students who do want to start their own businesses, now or later when they become adults, developing an understanding of entrepreneurship and also an entrepreneurial mindset is essential for realizing success in life and for the advancement of their careers, no matter what career path is chosen.

Before deciding whether entrepreneurship education is a schooling reform worth pursuing, it was worthwhile to listen to the words and views of high school students. The reason for this concern is that it is important to know what teenagers thought of business ownership, what they knew about entrepreneurship, markets and government, whether they wanted more instruction in these areas, and if so, what instruction was needed. No matter how much economists might argue for increased investment to improve the human capital of young people and the potential for increased social and economic productivity that will result from it, educational reform in that direction will go nowhere if the intended recipients lack interest.

To investigate such questions for this book, a detailed survey was constructed and administered to over 1,000 high school students across the United States. In addition, two other surveys were constructed and data were collected from a national sample of general public and a national sample of owners of small businesses so their responses could be compared with the voices of high school students. The details of the survey preparation and survey sampling are not the present focus of this chapter, so that explanation will be deferred to later sections of the chapter. For now, what needs to be reported are a few key findings from the high school survey to highlight what will be presented in greater detail in subsequent chapters.

What the interviews revealed was a widespread interest among high school students, and a resounding call, especially among minority youth, for educational change to provide more access to entrepreneurship education in the nation's schools. The results showed not only an interest among young people in starting for-profit and non-profit ventures, but also included the reasons for the interest in entrepreneurship among teenagers, what they possess in terms of entrepreneurial knowledge and skills, how they view the role of business owners in the community, and how their attitudes and knowledge changed over time. The survey findings support the main argument of this book: adding an entrepreneurship component to the school curriculum would give all youth the foundation to use entrepreneurial thinking in any line of work, and help many of them become entrepreneurs, thus contributing to personal success and the advancement of the economy.

In interviewing high school students from across the United States and listening to their voices regarding their own plans for their economic futures and their views of the motivations of business owners, the civic responsibilities of entrepreneurs, the role of government in regulating and taxing businesses and the kind of education these interested students would like to receive from the public school system, what kind of messages did they deliver? Although they were critical of business owners and did not think they were doing enough to help their communities, many teenagers today do not believe they can fulfill their dreams and positively affect their communities by taking the kind of jobs they see on limited offer around them. Instead, these young people recognize that if they want to effect change, improve their own conditions and the conditions in their communities, they have to make their own economic futures through some form of entrepreneurship. Unfortunately, they don't know how to do that and, moreover, they are aware of their own lack of knowledge and are eager for opportunities to acquire it.

THE MANY BENEFITS OF ENTREPRENEURSHIP

Increased entrepreneurship and more entrepreneurial thinking among the young people in the United States would have a number of benefits. Some of the positive effects of entrepreneurship are personal, intrinsic or individual, and they accrue to entrepreneurs economically, socially, and psychologically. Other benefits are more properly categorized as concomitant social or economic benefits; they enhance the general level of productivity in an economy, create more wealth and increase incomes, and improve the access to economic opportunity and the ownership of resources.

Most people would recognize that the most direct benefactor of business operation and ownership is the business owner. Even an entrepreneur who fails to succeed in business, closes a company, and moves on to something else, arguably gains in experience from the process of having initiated and operated a business. Doubtless the process of opening and operating a small business is a great educational experience. Among other qualities, it gives young entrepreneurs a chance to learn independence, financial skills and responsibility, salesmanship, business strategy, cooperation, leadership and the important skill discussed at the start of this chapter of being able both to *recognize* and *act* on opportunities. It also helps them better understand how the real world works: that is, how goods and services get from point "a" to point "b," why a product is packaged and priced the way it is, and what people mean when they debate laws or taxes that affect businesses.

The successful business also leads to income and prosperity for its owner. Business owners, in general, have the ability to grow according to their own capabilities and the conditions of the markets. In contrast, wage earners are subject to the prevailing wages, which are inherently limited. Starting a business, however, involves risk, and success is not assured whereas wage earners assume less risk and may have more stability if the job continues.

But in addition to the inherent personal benefits to the entrepreneur, increased entrepreneurship among young people confers benefits on society as well. Empowering young people to make their own jobs is good social policy because not only are these youth more likely to be upwardly mobile, they also are more likely to be involved as change agents in their communities, to innovate, to create jobs, to pay higher taxes, and to be engaged politically and solve social problems. It may be that business owners of all ages are more likely to vote than wage or salary earners.[4]

Arguably as important as increased individual well-being, social mobility, youth empowerment, and civic engagement is the role that small firms play in business innovation.[5] Most firms created by young entrepreneurs are small in size for the obvious reason that they are new and have not yet fully matured. Interestingly, small firms tend to drive innovation in the economy by producing products that fundamentally change how we live. The airplane, the FM radio and the personal computer all are examples of products that were first developed by small firms. Often these products eventually are sold to large corporations, which successfully adapt, market, and distribute them to consumers. This symbiotic relationship between small, innovative businesses and giant firms is not accidental. The distribution of innovation and dissemination between types of firms is a result of the market mechanism and is an indispensable part of a thriving economy.[6]

Economists also have noticed that small businesses create the most new jobs in our economy. Although this observation is not without controversy based on the size of firms and other factors, the current research consensus concurs that small businesses are the primary drivers of job growth in the United States. Small firms apparently experience more job volatility and loss than do large firms, thereby exerting a negative effect on employment, but small firms also tend to create the most new jobs simply because they are new firms, which tend to exhibit rapid growth rates.[7]

In addition, the creation of new firms replaces old firms that die and thus provide the needed vitality for communities, states, and regions in the United States. It is through this process of birth and renewal that entrepreneurship contributes to economic growth throughout the nation.[8] Getting youth to think about and act on their inclinations to start business firms will be critical for maintaining this dynamism and spark for economic growth in the economies of communities, states, and regions in the nation. Such economic growth that gets stimulated from the expansion of entrepreneurship becomes vital for nations to be able to compete and adapt to technological change in a global economy.[9]

OPPORTUNITY FOR ALL YOUTH

Not only do entrepreneurs in general benefit from owning their own businesses, but the personal advantages of entrepreneurship are greater, relative to wage earning, for young people who live in communities where taking a job is either a poor option, or is not an option at all. Business ownership may provide a potential route out of poverty for low-income populations who face a lack of opportunities in their communities or discrimination in the workplace.[10] There is growing recognition among government agencies and philanthropic organizations that entrepreneurship and its related activities may be a viable way to improve people's lives in low-income and blighted areas of communities. That is one reason why such organizations have encouraged the creation of "micro-enterprises" in these areas, and provide assistance or set-asides to minority-owned businesses.[11]

The provision of more entrepreneurship education would offer particular benefit to students from low-income communities for whom entrepreneurship is often the optimal strategy for economic and social mobility. One of the great purposes of secondary education in the United States is to provide for all young people an "alternative inheritance." Many teenagers, who are from low-income households, minority groups, immigrant communities, inner-city neighborhoods, or rural communities, have limited access to opportunities to increase their income and socioeconomic status. Excelling in the school competition for grades can be a path for some youths into a professional career, but for many youth, entrepreneurship also should be an option.

Most high schools typically avoid education for careers, especially the type that prepares youth for eventual self-employment or business ownership. In general, occupational or vocational programs have been relegated to non-college preparatory tracks, associated with lower-quality secondary education, and, at any rate, have focused on preparing students to work as *employees* in the skilled trades. Future *employers* receive their preparation elsewhere, often from their families or family connections. One tangible way schools could improve their students' future prospects would be to teach teenagers how to create ventures that employ themselves and others. Because this kind of instruction not only would provide the disadvantaged with enhanced access to entrepreneurial thinking and behavior, it would also help to level the playing field upon which access to society's economic benefits are determined, and therefore advance the goals of social equity along with the goals of the entrepreneurial spirit.

A historic purpose of schooling has been to enable upward social mobility.[12] One reason taxpayers are willing to subsidize the public schools in the United States partly has to do with the idea that public education is the way for youth to do better socially and economically when they become adults. Of course, schools also prepare children for citizenship responsibilities, and schools impart essential knowledge and develop skills related to literacy, numeracy, critical thinking, science, history, and other topics. All of this knowledge and these skills are intended, however, to help transform children into productive adults who are capable of pursuing their dreams and improving their standards of living.

There are several reasons schools need to provide this education for entrepreneurial thinking and entrepreneurship. First, schools are mainly oriented toward producing future wage earners and not future "job makers," and thus are not providing their students with the tools they need to access the means of production in the economy. Teenagers clearly are active on the consumption side of the economy, and that consumption has accelerated dramatically in recent years. Marketers and advertisers target teenagers as a demographic group that spends considerable amounts of money.[13]

This development is both positive and negative. It is positive because it indicates that young people have more money to spend, and this spending contributes to economic growth. It is negative because much of this spending is from household income or wealth, or access to credit cards, and it is money they did not earn. Even if students have a part-time job, the income often is being used to support a consumption lifestyle. In spending money they did not earn, or earning money from part-time jobs and then quickly spending it, teens are learning how to consume, but not to invest, budget, produce, or create wealth for their future.[14] The lack of emphasis on business ownership and entrepreneurial thinking and the deferred discussion of careers in the schools arguably put young people in a *consumption* rather than *production* state of mind. Entrepreneurs, by contrast, control their means of production.

A second reason for the need for more entrepreneurship education in the schools is that high school students who go through the educational system today will emerge into an economy that offers fewer chances to prosper through taking jobs than has been the case in the past. Recent economic changes, linked to globalization and technology, among other factors, make entrepreneurship and enterprise initiatives increasingly important components of the U.S. economy. With some exceptions, jobs in manufacturing are declining, service sector jobs often offer low wages, and opportunities for agriculture are vanishing as family or small farms disappear.[15] In cities, less advantaged youth lack access to the kinds of jobs their peers occupy in more affluent parts of the city. An additional alarming development has been the migration or outsourcing of jobs to other nations in both low-wage and high-wage industries in the U.S. economy.

During the last two decades, increases in real wages for wage and salary workers at the bottom of the wage distribution have not kept pace with increases for such workers at the top of the distribution. Additionally, there are greater disparities in household income between those at the top and bottom of the income distribution, even after adjustments for taxes and government payments. Also, increasing returns from capital investment have contributed to growing disparities in wealth. These trends are a major concern for society and are likely to continue into the foreseeable future.[16]

While many young people from more advantaged backgrounds may have the option of going into a profession or occupation with the opportunity to earn a high income, for many high school students who live in inner cities or poorer rural areas, following such a career path is not a realistic option. Making a job, by initiating a for-profit or not-for-profit venture is a potentially better strategy, and sometimes the only opportunity for breaking the poverty cycle. But without the knowledge and skills to pursue access to the means of production, many youth educated in the schools will have to compete on a tilted playing field outside of school that dramatically hinders their ability to achieve autonomous production and higher levels of income.

Therefore, the nation's schools need to do more to encourage, enhance, and expand entrepreneurship education. This instruction would help all youth, regardless of background or circumstances, acquire the entrepreneurial skills, knowledge and habits of mind to initiate ventures, innovate in their business practices, create jobs, produce wealth, and in the long run, give back to their communities. Schools that add preparation for entrepreneurship to their education functions would ensure that all students have the opportunity to capture the personal benefits, and they also would increase the social and economic benefits that come from new venture creation.

With these themes in mind, the attention turns to the surveys and data. The discussion focuses on the methods used to find the entrepreneur in youth.

SURVEYS, SAMPLES, AND METHODS

The surveys used to collect the data for the book were designed and validated by the authors (Kourilsky and Walstad).[17] They were administered by The Gallup Organization under controlled protocols to national samples of U.S. high school students, members of the general public (hereafter general public), and owners of small businesses with 50 or fewer employees.

Questionnaire development entailed specification of content, writing and ordering questions, and extensive review and revision. In this process, valuable comments on the questions were obtained from reviews by experts in business, entrepreneurship, economics, and education to help establish the reliability and validity of items for each survey. Five drafts of the survey were prepared in the process of survey development.

On the final two drafts the authors worked with staff members at The Gallup Organization with extensive expertise in survey development. These individuals offered suggestions for changes, corrected for any wording problems or biases, provided technical review of items, and checked each survey for public release. The last draft of each survey was given a careful proofing and also was field-tested or reviewed to check the appropriate length and the validity of item use with the samples surveyed. (The survey questions used for analysis can be found in the tables and text of this book.)

The Gallup Organization selected the samples of high school students, the general public, and owners of small businesses using its survey procedures. The three surveys were administered by The Gallup Organization through telephone interviews in the fall of 2002. Survey responses were entered into the computer at the time of survey administration. The responses to open-ended questions were coded and edited by Gallup personnel who specialize in this phase of telephone survey research. Gallup personnel summarized the data, which was then analyzed and interpreted by the authors. The authors then conducted the data analysis for each survey and provided the interpretation of all survey results reported in this book based on the three data sets provided by The Gallup Organization.[18]

It should be noted that the core contents of the three surveys have a long history of use, which contributes to establishing the reliability of the survey items and the general validity of the findings. The original work to prepare the three surveys actually began in 1993. The surveys were first administered by The Gallup Organization in the spring of 1994 to the three national random samples of U.S. high school students, the U.S. general public, and owners of U.S. small businesses. In the subsequent years, the original surveys were modified as necessary by the authors for use with other groups. For these later surveys, slight revisions were made to some questions, other questions were omitted, and new questions were added, but a core of the original survey questions remained in use. The authors then arranged to have the surveys administered by The Gallup Organization to national random samples of other groups in various years: (1) youth, ages 14–19, in 1995; (2) young adults, ages 14–39, in 1996; (3) teachers in elementary school, and business and social studies teachers in middle schools and high schools in 1997; (4) teachers again in 1998 to study technology issues; and (5) owners of high-technology businesses in 2001.[19] For the purposes of this book, many of the questions on the 2002 survey had been used with each sample in 1994, thus providing the opportunity to conduct a longitudinal analysis from 1994 to 2002 on a subset of items, the findings from which will be presented in a later chapter in the book.

High School Students

Gallup survey procedures were used to select each household in which to interview a high school student. Within each contacted household, an interview was sought with the high school student with the most recent birthday. To qualify, a student must have been in ninth, tenth, eleventh, or twelfth grade during the 2002–2003 school year. This method of respondent selection within households produces an age distribution that closely approximates the age distribution of the total population.

Multiple calls were made to each selected telephone number to complete an interview. The time and the day of the week for callbacks were varied to maximize the chances of finding a respondent at home. All high school interviews were conducted on weekday evenings or weekends when high school students would likely be at home. Only one complete interview per household was obtained. The surveying was conducted from September 12 to October 17, 2002. For the high school sample, there were a total of 1,010 completed interviews that were used for this study. The data were weighted by The Gallup Organization based on national norms that included such factors as age, gender, race, ethnicity, and region of the country.[20]

General Public

The Gallup Organization drew a random sample of the general public from the continental United States. A three-call design was used in which at least up to three calls were made to each possible respondent in efforts to reach more than just the "easy to reach" portion of the population. Gallup also used a random-digit-dial (RDD) technique to ensure inclusion of both listed and unlisted telephone numbers.

Interviews with the general public were conducted from September 17 to October 17, 2002. A total of 607 interviews were completed with the general public. The data were weighted by The Gallup Organization based on national norms that included age, gender, race, ethnicity, education, income, and region of the country.

Small Business Owners

The sample of small business owners was randomly drawn by The Gallup Organization from a listing of businesses stratified by geographic location and industry. The listing excluded non-profit organizations or government agencies. The business firms also had to employ fewer than 50 employees. A disproportionate sample design was used to set quotas of one-third for each of three employee ranges: 1–9, 10–19, and 20–49. The overall data from all business owners were then weighted back to the actual distribution of companies based on the universe of business firms.

Only the owner of the small business was surveyed. Up to five calls were made to each telephone number in order to complete an interview. Business owners were telephoned during business hours and interview appointments were made when necessary. The surveying was conducted from September 9 to October 11, 2002. A total of 403 business owners completed interviews for the study.

Sample Characteristics

The basic demographics for the three samples are reported in Table 1.1. The table shows both the weighted and unweighted results, but the weighted percentages were the ones used for the analysis. Males constituted 50% of the high school sample, 48% of the general public sample, and the overwhelming proportion (73%) of the business owner sample.

The samples showed some differences in terms of the race and ethnicity of the groups. When asked about their race, two-thirds (67%) of the high school

The Entrepreneur in Youth

Table 1.1 Sample Characteristics

Characteristic	High School Students		General Public		Business Owners	
	Un-weighted	Weighted	Un-weighted	Weighted	Un-weighted	Weighted
	(n=1010)	(1,010)	(607)	(607)	(403)	(403)
	%	%	%	%	%	%
Gender						
Male	44	51	42	48	73	73
Female	55	50	58	52	27	27
Race						
White	55	67	82	80	89	85
African American	22	15	8	9	4	4
Hispanic	17	12	3	4	3	4
Asian	4	4	3	3	1	2
Other	2	2	4	4	4	7
Hispanic origin						
Yes	20	14	5	6	4	6
No	70	85	93	92	96	94
Location						
Northeast	12	17	19	19	15	14
South Central	47	36	35	36	35	36
North Central	25	25	27	23	30	26
West	16	22	20	22	20	24
Education: Youth						
Ninth grade	10	22	–	–	–	–
Tenth grade	21	27	–	–	–	–
Eleventh grade	31	26	–	–	–	–
Twelfth grade	38	26	–	–	–	–
Education: Others						
1st–11th grades	–	–	8	10	3	3
High school graduate	–	–	28	34	18	20
Some college	–	–	25	27	26	25
Four-year graduate	–	–	21	14	32	33
Post college graduate	–	–	15	10	19	17
Vocational/other	–	–	4	5	3	3
Income						
< $25,000	–	–	27	29	–	–
$25,000 to < $50,000	–	–	30	31	–	–
$50,000 to < $75,000	–	–	14	13	–	–
$75,000 to $100,000+	–	–	20	18	–	–
Age (average in years)	16	16	45	44	50	51
Age (median in years)	16	16	43	43	50	49

sample stated they were white, but eight in ten (80%) of the general public and almost nine in ten (89%) owners of small businesses said they were white. African Americans composed 15% of the high school students, 9% of the general public sample, and just 4% of small business owners. When asked whether they were of Hispanic origin, 20% of the high school students said yes, but only 6% of the other groups said yes.

The regional distribution for the samples was relatively similar. The largest regional group (36%) of high school students came from the South Central region of the United States, as was the case with the general public and small business owners. A quarter (25%) of high school students came from the North Central region, about the same percentage as the general public (23%) and business owners (26%). The West was the location for more than two in ten of each group, and the Northeast was the location for less than two in ten of each group.

Various levels of education were reported for each sample. The general public sample had 34% who reported only graduating from high school, but 10% did not graduate from high school. Another 27% were those with some college education, including those who were two-year college graduates. Four-year college graduates and those with postgraduate work accounted for 24% of the general public sample. A fifth (20%) of business owners were high school graduates and a quarter (25%) had some college work, but half (50%) were either four-year college graduates (33%) or had taken postgraduate work (17%). High school students, of course, were in grades nine (22%), ten (27%), eleven (26%), and twelve (26%).

In terms of age, the high school students had an average age of 16 years. By contrast, the average age was 44 years for the general public with a median of 43 years, and an average age of 51 years for owners of small businesses with a median of 49 years.

Although not reported in Table 1.1, employment data were collected on high school students and the general public. Thirty percent (30%) of the high school sample were employed in part-time jobs whereas about two-thirds (62%) of the general public were employed. Among the employed youth, about a quarter (23%) worked less than 10 hours a week; about half (51%) worked 10 to 20 hours a week, and about a quarter (25%) worked 21 or more hours a week. Among the employed general public, 23% worked less than 35 hours, 36% worked 36 to 40 hours, and 40% worked more than 40 hours. For the general public, the type of work cited most often was professional employee (22%), service worker (17%), or skilled craft worker (12%). Being a manager, a clerical worker, a sales worker, or an operative each accounted for about one in ten (9 to 10%) of those working.

The final demographic worth noting is for owners of small businesses and the size of their firms. The unweighted sample for this group was divided into thirds based on three employee ranges: 1–9, 10–19, and 20–49. When these data were weighted, almost nine in ten (88%) of these small businesses only had 1–10 employees. The remaining 12% of firms either had 11–19 employees (7%) or 20–49 employees (5%). The owners of most small businesses who were surveyed have small operations because the vast majority of these firms have less than 10 employees.

Response Rates and Sampling Error

The response rates for the samples were generally acceptable and similar to those conducted with such samples by national firms specializing in survey research of this type. The response rate was 18% for the total potential group of high school respondents, 20% of the total potential group of general public respondents, and 28% of the total potential group of small business respondents.

At the 95% level of confidence, the maximum expected range of the sampling error for the sample of 1,010 high school students would be plus or minus (+/–) 3.1 percentage points. In the case of the general public of 607, the maximum margin of sampling error would be +/– 4.0 percentage points. For the sample of 403 owners of small businesses, the maximum margin of sampling error would be +/– 4.9 percentage points.

Using the general public as an example, the maximum margin of the sampling error means that if 100 different samples of 607 persons from the general public were randomly chosen, then 95 times out of 100, the sample results obtained would vary by no more than +/– 4.0 percentage points. Of course, the maximum margin of sampling error applies to those responses of about 50%. For a sample of 607 and an item response of 10% or 90%, the sampling error falls to about +/– 1.9 percentage points. The margin of sampling error for each survey and item response, therefore, just gives the reader a guide for gauging the expected range of survey response.

To keep the presentation of the results manageable, the discussion of sampling error and any tests for statistical significance will not be used in reporting the results in this book. Statistical significance does provide a useful guide for assessing whether the difference of one reported percentage from another is large and not just due to chance, but it is just a guide and the outcomes can be influenced by many factors. The designation of statistical significance can be changed by such factors as the selected level of confidence (90, 95, or 99%), the expected direction of the difference (using a one-tailed or two-tailed test), the sample size, and the percentage of the responses to items. It is sufficient for the purposes of this book to indicate when differences in percentage responses are large and likely to be important or meaningful, but it is not important to use statistical significance, however defined, as the absolute measure of what to report or discuss.[21]

There is a final reason for avoiding the strict use of statistical testing for the analysis and reports of the survey results. In any survey, other errors beyond sampling may have been introduced as a result of question order and wording, interview bias, and non-response, among other possible factors. The bias in the reported findings as a result of these error sources is difficult, if not impossible, to estimate.

ORGANIZATION OF THE BOOK

Chapter 2 presents the main results of the study that quantify the interest in entrepreneurship among this nation's young people. This interest begins early in life and can be nurtured to advance entrepreneurship. Differences in interest emerge between young men and women and between high school students in general and minority groups, both African American youth and Hispanic youth, whose interest in starting their own businesses is notably high. This chapter also includes a discussion of the reasons for students' interests and the formative experiences that lead them to contemplate starting their own ventures. These results are compared to the responses to the same questions that were asked of the general public and small business owners.

Not only are young people interested in owning and operating their own businesses – mainly because they want to be their own bosses – but also because they want to "give back." This generation of young people has a strong sense of civic and social responsibility and has been termed Generation E – the generation that combines an entrepreneurial spirit with a community or social mindset.[22] Chapter 3 presents results from survey questions about teenage attitudes toward philanthropy and contributing to the community. The evidence is clear that, when compared to current small business owners, young people believe it is more important to contribute to their community in some way. They do not believe that businesses in general contribute in ways that extend beyond creating jobs and, like members of the general public, high school students believe business owners generally give back in ways that promote their own businesses. Probably the most remarkable finding is the level of interest that young people have in creating not-for-profit ventures that help their communities: close to two-thirds of youth declared their desire to do so, whereas well under half of the general public and closer to one-third of business owners have similar intentions.

Despite this interest in independent work and helping the community, relatively few young people actually realize their aspirations by establishing their own ventures. The findings of this study suggest that this low rate of companies founded by youth may be a result of a number of barriers young entrepreneurs face in U.S. society. The next three chapters in the book (4, 5, and 6) explore these important obstacles to developing and enhancing the entrepreneurial spirit and inclination of youth.

One of the barriers is that high school students have a low level of confidence in their own knowledge. They rate themselves as having much to learn, and think they are deficient in their preparation to start a business. When asked a series of questions concerning business or entrepreneurship and also economics, they reveal their significant lack of knowledge and understanding of basic concepts and ideas that help prepare people for entrepreneurship. Chapter 4 discusses the findings on high school students' knowledge of entrepreneurship and business practices, and explains how this low level of achievement and confidence serves as a major obstacle to the ability to act on entrepreneurial aspirations.

Chapter 5 presents data that show high school students hold opinions about the functioning of competitive markets and the role of government that are dissonant with their interest in pursuing entrepreneurship. Although most young people like the outcomes from competitive markets that they see and experience as consumers, they often criticize businesses and enterprises for decisions that are driven by market consideration, and they often support government intervention in the processes that define competitive markets. This chapter discusses the confusing views of young people about the production side of the economy, and how the views often reflect a lack of understanding about how markets function. The chapter also considers the potentially negative effects of such views, taken in the aggregate, on the entrepreneurial aspirations and success of the young people who have these opinions, and their potentially inhibitory implications for starting businesses and supporting the entrepreneurial economy.

The last barrier young entrepreneurs face, as discussed in Chapter 6, is perhaps the most important, but also the most tractable. High school students in the United States today do not participate for the most part in any kind of entrepreneurship education. They want this kind of instructional experience and recognize its potential value, but they may never receive it in their education in high school or, for that matter, outside of high school. Furthermore, they may not be trained for entrepreneurship after they graduate from high school, if they do graduate, because not everyone goes on to postsecondary education, and even if they do attend a college, university, or some other postsecondary institution, they may not have the opportunity to receive instruction that prepares them for entrepreneurship. A feasible opportunity for preparing all youth (and future adults) to participate in an entrepreneurial economy is during the high school years.

Chapter 6 reports that young people are demanding more entrepreneurship education. It also describes how this type of educational service is one of the major forces for expanding entrepreneurship. The chapter presents survey responses and analysis data on the attitudes and experiences of high school students with respect to different modes of delivery for this entrepreneurship education. It explores what type of education young people need to identify opportunities, marshal resources in the face of risk, and initiate and operate entrepreneurial ventures in the not-for-profit, for-profit, and public sectors of the economy. It also discusses approaches for reorienting school philosophies and curricula to accommodate and provide such education.

A reasonable question to be asked after all the data and results that are presented is whether the survey findings are consistent with past studies of youth entrepreneurship, or whether they are somehow unique to the year the survey was administered, and therefore are an exception to past findings. That issue is investigated in the first part of Chapter 7. Fortunately, many of the results from the 2002 survey that were reported in the previous five chapters can be compared with findings from a previous survey of high school students, the general public, and small business owners that was conducted in 1994. The general conclusion is that most of the previous findings still hold and are consistent with those found when analyzing the most recent survey, thus helping to reinforce the prior findings and also helping to establish the validity of the more recent results.

Once this longitudinal perspective is presented, the data analysis and reporting are complete, and the second part of Chapter 7 turns to a presentation of the major findings. Of course, findings and conclusions are presented in each of the five previous chapters, but given the vast array of data it is easy to get lost in all the details and therefore miss the major points. It is valuable to have a certain amount of repetition or restatement of the findings and conclusions, in case for one reason or another, they were somehow missed or overlooked by the reader and so the reader does not have to continuously refer to an earlier chapter. What the end of Chapter 7 offers is a concise and clear statement of the major findings and conclusions, so they are highlighted and given sufficient emphasis.

Chapter 8, the last chapter of this book, uses the major findings and conclusions from the data analysis as the basis for a broader interpretation and explanation of their meaning and insights. The chapter draws extensive implications and makes extrapolations from the results that are presented for the five key topics in prior chapters: (1) interest in entrepreneurship;

(2) giving back to the community and philanthropy; (3) knowledge and understanding of entrepreneurship; (4) opinions about markets and government; and (5) entrepreneurship education.

These implications and extrapolations become the basis for a set of recommendations for expanding and enhancing entrepreneurship education and entrepreneurial experiences for today's high school youth – the all-important talent pool from which entrepreneurial thinkers and venture initiators of tomorrow will be drawn. The goal should be to work toward bridging the gap for young people between entrepreneurial interest and the pursuit of entrepreneurial venture initiation. Success with respect to that goal will better enable all young people, regardless of background or life experiences, to translate their interest and enthusiasm into control of their means of production for starting their own enterprises and for pursuing initiatives to improve communities and society.

NOTES

1. Burt (1992), p. 274.
2. See www.blackgirlmagazineonline.com.
3. For an example of such books, see Kantor (2006) or Swartz (2006).
4. The U.S. Census (2002) has reported that people who feel more invested in the society – older people, homeowners and marrieds, people with higher income, higher education and jobs – have the highest rate of voting participation (www.census.gov/prod/2002pubs/p20-542.pdf). Also, one organization commissioned a nationwide poll in 2003 and found voter participation among women entrepreneurs to be 90%, which is higher than the rates for any group defined by the Census report (www.wipp.org).
5. Acs and Audretsch (1988).
6. See Baumol (2005).
7. Birch (1987) may have been the first economist to document that small businesses are the primary drivers of job growth in the United States. Davis, Haltiwanger, and Schuh (1996) and Bednarzik (2000) both challenged this conclusion by arguing that small firms experience more job volatility and loss than do large firms. Haltiwanger and Krizan (1999) found the picture to be more complicated; small firms tend to create the most new jobs simply because they are new firms, which also tend to exhibit rapid growth rates. The manufacturing sector is an exception to this phenomenon. Examining the situation from a regional perspective, Acs and Armington (2004) found that small businesses contribute to new employment growth on a region-to-region basis. And

in a review of the scholarship, Karlsson, Friis, and Paulsson (2006) found substantial evidence from studies conducted all over the globe for the importance of small businesses in economic growth and job creation.

8. See Bruce, Deskins, Hill, and Rork (2007) for an analysis of the effect of small business on economic growth in states.

9. See Carree and Thurik (2006) for studies on the relationship between entrepreneurship and economic growth, and in particular, Wennekers and Thurik (1999) in that volume.

10. Fairlie (2004) asked whether young people from low-income families who started their own businesses experienced higher earnings than similar people who were wage and salary workers. His results indicated that young men (but not women) business owners from disadvantaged backgrounds earned more on average than their counterparts who worked for others. The difference between the two groups was large, significant, and comparable to the effect that the level of parent education exerts on income. That this increase in earnings did not apply to women is in all likelihood explained by the nature of the self-employment these women typically experienced. Probably more often than men, women worked part time, perhaps out of their homes, and engaged in earnings activities while also raising children.

11. For examples, see Severens and Kays (1999).

12. Katz (1989), pp. 21–22.

13. For example, a survey conducted by Teenager Research Unlimited (www.teenresearch.com) estimated that U.S. teenagers spent $159 billion of their own money or their parents' or guardians' money in 2005.

14. Perhaps this pattern of spending is partly accountable for why only 32% of teenagers reported in one survey that they knew how to budget money (web.mit.edu/invent/n-pressreleases/n-press-06index.html). More generally, the Federal Reserve System, government agencies, and non-profit organizations have addressed the need for more financial literacy among youth (e.g., Braunstein and Welch 2002).

15. According to the U.S. Census Bureau (2005), the number of manufacturing establishments declined by 12,094 between 1997 and 2002. Jobs in this sector decreased by 3,400,845 between 1997 and 2004. In farming, between 1997 and 2002, the number of farms in the United States fell by almost 87,000 (U.S. Department of Agriculture 2004).

16. For a discussion of trends and concerns in the level and distribution of economic well-being in the U.S. economy, see Bernanke (2007).

17. See Walstad (1994), Walstad and Kourilsky (1996), and Walstad and Kourilsky (1999) for descriptions of the prior history in the 1994 survey and the basic results.

18. Given the extensive amount of data collected from each survey, not all data results from each survey item are presented in this book.
19. More detailed information about the content of these questionnaires, and additional data and analysis, can be found in previously published articles and books. See Walstad (1994), Walstad and Kourilsky (1996), Walstad and Kourilsky (1999), Kourilsky and Walstad (2000), Kourilsky and Walstad (2002), and Kourilsky and Walstad (2005).
20. Of the 1,010 high school students surveyed, about 600 were randomly drawn from the general population of high school students. In addition, there were completed interviews of 200 identified Hispanic high school students and 200 identified African American high school students. These interviews came from a listed sample where the race and ethnicity were self-reported by the respondents. The reason for this over-sampling of African American and Hispanic youth was to ensure that these groups were of sufficient size for sub-sample reporting of any results.
21. The necessary information is also reported for the survey responses so that the reader can conduct such a statistical test for differences should that be important.
22. Kourilsky and Walstad (2000).

2. Interest in Entrepreneurship

The "spirit of entrepreneurship" is a vital part of the American dream. It is derived from the belief that individuals can improve their standard of living and control their destiny. Since the founding of the nation, the opportunities to start businesses and make them successful have been a driving force for growth in the economy, technological advancement, and the fulfillment of the economic aspirations of people.

A major purpose of this chapter is to investigate the degree to which the spirit of entrepreneurship was found in the thinking of high school students in the United States in the first decade of the twenty-first century. Many high school students, who will soon become adults, have a strong desire to take control of their lives and build something for themselves. Entrepreneurship is a natural avenue for channeling that energy and motivation, and this avenue only widens as these youth grow and mature.

INITIAL INTEREST

Two major questions were included on the survey to gauge the interest in entrepreneurship among high school students. The first question examined students' preferences for starting a business versus working for someone else. Regardless of what the current condition or personal situation that the young respondents were facing in their lives, the first question posed a hypothetical choice. It asked: "If you had the choice between starting your own business, or work for someone else who owns a business, which would you rather do?"

The responses to the first question show there is great interest in entrepreneurship among high school students (Table 2.1). If given this entrepreneurial choice, almost two-thirds of high school students (64%) would rather start their own businesses than work for someone else. This percentage is remarkable given the very daunting challenges that starting a business presents for the aspiring entrepreneur.

Table 2.1 Starting Own Business or Work for Someone Else[a]

Response	Total (n=1010)	Male (444)	Female (566)	White (639)	African American (232)	Hispanic (205)
	High School Students					
	%	%	%	%	%	%
Starting own business	64	66	61	60	77	75
Working for someone else	34	31	37	38	23	23
Neither	0	0	0	0	–	–
Both	2	2	1	2	0	2
Don't know/Refused	1	1	–	1	0	0

Note: [a]"Thinking about business, if you had the choice between starting your own business or working for someone else who owns a business, which would you rather do?"

Of course, the naiveté of high school students about what is required to start and run a business accounts for some of this interest. Without having experienced the challenges of initiating a business venture and not being acquainted with role models of entrepreneurs, most of the respondents probably cannot appreciate the difficulty and frustration of turning a business idea into reality. Nevertheless, the responses suggest that the entrepreneurial desire is clearly lodged in the minds of U.S. youth even if some of it stems from naiveté. Also, it is also not a passing fancy, as later evidence reported in this chapter and the other chapters in this book will reveal.

There is ample evidence that women-owned businesses are becoming a dominant force in the economy.[1] A 2002 census survey reported that there were 6.5 million businesses owned by women and they accounted for 28.2% of all non-farm firms in the United States. About 14% of these women-owned firms had employees. They employed 7.1 million workers and had an annual payroll of $173.7 billion. From 1997 to 2002, the number of women-owned businesses also grew at a faster rate than the number of businesses overall (19.8% for women-owned businesses versus 10.3% for all businesses). These data suggest that it is important to examine gender differences in entrepreneurship to see if there is a strong interest among female youth that will continue to fuel the trend toward women ownership of businesses in the U.S. economy.

The responses from high school females verify that there is strong interest in entrepreneurship among the next generation of females. At least six in ten (61%) female youth would rather start a business than work for someone else. Less than four in ten (37%) wanted to work for someone else. On this question, the percentage responses for females and males were similar. If given a choice, about the same percentage of females and males would opt for the entrepreneurship route, which suggests that females do not consider entrepreneurship to be primarily a male career option. The females' responses are encouraging for entrepreneurship in the United States. They suggest that there is a large potential pool of female youth who may decide to choose a career path in entrepreneurship, thus increasing the number of women-owned businesses in the future.[2]

Economic statistics also show that the number of businesses owned by minorities is a major force in the economy.[3] In 2002, there were 1.2 million firms owned by African Americans and these firms accounted for 5.2% of all non-farm businesses. In addition, there were 1.6 million firms owned by Hispanics and they represented 6.8% of all nonfarm businesses. In the five-year period (1997 to 2002) covered by the survey, the growth of firms owned by African Americans and Hispanics increased at significantly faster rates than that for all businesses (45.4% for firms owned by African Americans and 31.1% for firms owned by Hispanics compared with 10.3% for all businesses). Given the sizable business ownership and significant growth in entrepreneurship among African Americans and Hispanics in recent years, the youth responses also were studied for differences by race and ethnicity.

A brief explanation is necessary, however, to understand how the sample was subdivided by race and ethnicity. Gallup used three demographic questions to classify the race and ethnicity of respondents. One question asked the respondents to state their race ("What is your race? Are you white, African American, or some other race?"). A second question asked about their ethnicity ("Are you, yourself, of Hispanic origin or descent, such as Mexican, Puerto Rican, Cuban, or other Spanish background?"). Those respondents who stated they were Hispanic were asked a third question about whether they would classify themselves as a white-Hispanic or a black-Hispanic. The main self-reported categories for race with sufficient data for subgroup reporting were white and African American. The total for whites (n=639) includes 84 respondents who reported Hispanic as their race, but in the next question stated they were a white-Hispanic. The total for African American (n=232) includes 13 respondents who reported Hispanic as their race, but in the next question stated that they were a black-Hispanic. The remaining respondents (n=139) from the total sample of 1,010 stated they were of another race (e.g., Asian) or they did not give a usable response.

The white and African American responses are directly comparable because they represent two unique categories. Care should be taken, however, in making strict comparisons between whites and Hispanics or between blacks and Hispanics because there is some overlap. The Hispanic category includes all respondents (n=205) who stated they were Hispanic in response to the Gallup question. In the next question some in the Hispanic group also identified themselves as a white-Hispanic (n=84) or a black-Hispanic (n=13), so the Hispanic category includes some representation from whites and African Americans.

The results show a strong interest in entrepreneurship among African American and Hispanic high school students. Over three-fourths (77%) of African American youth said they would rather start a business than work for someone else. This percentage was significantly higher by 17 percentage points than that for white youth (60%). The results for Hispanic youth were essentially equivalent to that for African American youth, with three-fourths (75%) saying they would select the choice of starting a business over working for someone else. These results strongly suggest that there is also a large pool of potential entrepreneurs among African American and Hispanic high school students, even at this relatively young age. The challenge is figuring out how to leverage this interest so it produces more access to entrepreneurship and entrepreneurial thinking for African Americans and Hispanics in the United States.[4]

The high school responses also can be compared with those from other groups – the general public and owners of small businesses. As with youth, the general public shows great interest in entrepreneurship. Almost two-thirds of the general public (64%) would take the entrepreneurship option over working for someone else if given the choice. One-third (33%) said they would prefer to work for someone else. This high percentage expressing interest in entrepreneurship is surprising because many of them have worked for, or are currently working for, someone else in a job. Perhaps, based on their own personal circumstances, employment situation, or life experiences, many currently view making a job for themselves as a preferable alternative to taking a job.

Among owners of small businesses, there was strong support for the entrepreneurial choice as might be expected because each of them had made such a choice at one point in their lives. If given the choice again, the great majority (85%) would take the entrepreneurial path again, and few (10%) regretted their previous decision and would say no. The percentages remain essentially at the same high level regardless of the number of people employed by the small business owner: 85% for those with 1–9 employees; 82% for those with 10–19 employees; and 86% for those with 20–49 employees. The high percentage of support for entrepreneurship indicates that there is a great amount of work and career satisfaction among this group.[5]

MORE INTEREST

Asking students hypothetically whether they would prefer to start their own business or work for another person produces information about students' relative preferences. Conceivably, if these young people were given the choice of *neither* having to start a business *nor* work for another person, many would have chosen that option. A stronger way to ascertain what young people might actually do with their productive energy would be to ask a more direct question. Accordingly, another question on the survey asked: "Do *you* want to start a business of your own?" Worded this way, the question presumably elicited responses that took into account respondents' current conditions or personal situations.

Responses to this more direct question (Table 2.2) also show considerable interest in entrepreneurship among U.S. youth. About two-thirds (65%) of high school students would like to start their own businesses, a percentage that is about the same as that for the first entrepreneurial interest question (Table 2.1).

Table 2.2 Want to Start Own Business[a]

| Response | High School Students | | | | | |
	Total (n=1010)	Male (444)	Female (566)	White (639)	African American (232)	Hispanic (205)
	%	%	%	%	%	%
Yes	65	72	58	63	75	70
No	33	26	40	36	23	28
Don't know/Refused	1	1	2	1	2	2

Note: [a]"Do you think you would want to start a business of your own?"

There was also a strong interest in entrepreneurship expressed among both male and female youth in response to this question about what youth actually want to do. The responses are generally consistent with the strong interest in entrepreneurship shown in the previous question that gave respondents an unconstrained choice to consider, but the results of the second question produced a more pronounced gap between male and female responses. Well over one in ten fewer high school females than males were interested in starting a business (58% versus 72%).[6]

Why this female–male difference arises is difficult to explain. It may be that there are gender-related differences in the risk-taking attitudes and behavior or other psychological factors related to entrepreneurship. Also, it may be that females are more aware of their knowledge deficiencies than males – a fact that may make them less confident in their ability to succeed in starting a business. Alternatively, males may have been overly confident of their abilities, given their actual level of knowledge. The question also arises as to whether youths' views of entrepreneurship are biased toward the male gender. The respondents may associate the qualities that they imagine to be essential for entrepreneurship with qualities in which males should excel. For example, if initiative is a quality associated with entrepreneurship and if studies show that females see males excelling in that quality, this might explain the female–male difference in the survey. These associations may arise from the media, upbringing, personal experiences of gender discrimination, and access. Instructional practices or curriculum content in school also may reduce the level of female interest in starting a business. These and other possible explanations will be addressed in later chapters because interest in entrepreneurship can affect the number of females who eventually start their own businesses.

The responses of white, African American, and Hispanic groups of high school youth to this question are about the same as the responses they gave to the previous questions. African Americans are the ones most interested in starting a business (75%), followed by Hispanics (70%), and then whites (63%). The gap between whites and African Americans remains sizable (12 percentage points). Hispanic interest in starting a business falls somewhat with this direct question compared with the choice question, but it is still at a very high level. The big conclusion from the African American and Hispanic responses to both questions is that there is indeed a high degree of interest among these groups that could be tapped to produce more minority entrepreneurs in the United States.

Unlike high school students, who responded with entrepreneurial zeal to both the more hypothetical and the more direct question about entrepreneurial interest, the general public responded slightly less positively to the second question about what they would actually do (55% total: 48% saying yes and 7% saying have already started) than the first question (64%). This difference most likely arises because some members of the general public are not in a position to act on their entrepreneurial inclinations. They are retired or have made other lifetime commitments that restrict their free choice that was assumed with the response to the first question.

A further analysis of the results from the general public to the second question clearly shows that the intensity of the entrepreneurial flame varies according to age. About two-thirds (68%) of those 42 years old or younger – who are in the prime years for entrepreneurship – said they would want to start a business of their own. Another 5% of this group already had started a business. Among those 43 or older, about one-third (34%) said they were interested in starting a business. Another 8% of this group said they had started one. Thus from a total perspective, about seven in ten (73%) of those 42 or younger showed interest in entrepreneurship compared with only about four in ten (42%) of those of age 43 or older.

LIKELIHOOD OF ENTREPRENEURSHIP

This interest in entrepreneurship is not a passing thought among high school students. Table 2.3 shows the responses of those high school students who said they wanted to start a business of their own and who answered a follow-up question on the likelihood of doing so. Over five in ten (54%) of these high school students also said they were either *very likely* (19%) or *likely* (35%) to act on the entrepreneurial idea. By contrast, less than one in ten (8%) of this group say they are *unlikely* (6%) or *not at all likely* (2%) to start a business. A sizable percentage (38%) of these high school students, however, expressed uncertainty about whether they will act. The significant uncertainty probably arises from the lack of thoughtful reflection on this topic. The low negative response to the question corroborates the likelihood that entrepreneurship remains a provocative idea that they have not fully fleshed out in their minds.[7] Overall, the responses indicate that these high school students will need help in the form of education or job experiences if

Table 2.3 Likely to Act on Idea to Start Own Business[a]

| Response | High School Students | | | | | |
	Total (n=664)[b]	Male (325)[b]	Female (339)[b]	White (398)[b]	African American (176)[b]	Hispanic (142)[b]
	%	%	%	%	%	%
5 Very likely	19	18	20	17	27	24
4	35	37	34	33	40	40
3	38	38	37	42	28	28
2	6	6	6	7	4	5
1 Not at all likely	2	1	3	1	1	3
Don't know/Refused	2	–	1	0	1	1

Notes:
[a]"Using a five-point scale, where 5 is very likely, and 1 is not at all likely, how likely are you to act on this idea to start your own business?"
[b]For YES respondents on whether you'd want to start a business of your own (see Table 2.2).

they are to act on their inclination. Chapter 6 discusses the education and training they are likely to need to develop their entrepreneurial interests into a reality worth embracing.

The responses of female and male high school students show little difference. Over five in ten females (54%) and males (55%) said they were *very likely* or *likely* to act on an idea to start a business. What is encouraging is that among the pool of high school youth interested in starting a business, few females (9%) or few males (8%) are saying that they were *not at all likely* or *unlikely* to act to start a business. There are, however, sizable proportions of females (37%) and males (38%) who are undecided about how likely they are to act. This group is one that might be highly influenced by more education and training in entrepreneurship to prepare them with more knowledge, skills, and confidence to make that decision.

As for differences by race and ethnicity, over six in ten (62%) of African American youth and over four in ten (41%) of Hispanic youth said they were *very likely* or *likely* to start a business. These responses are further indications of the great interest in entrepreneurship among these minority groups. These responses make it clear that the potential for entrepreneurship among minorities has yet to be fully realized. Especially in the case of Hispanic youth, the drop from stated interest in starting a business (70%) to being likely to act upon the interest (41%) demands consideration of the factors that discourage access to entrepreneurship and entrepreneurship knowledge and how these factors play out in a particular social and cultural context. Among white youth the response was about five in ten (52%) saying they were *very likely* or *likely* to act on the idea to start a business.

The results for the general public are similar to those for high school students, and are presented for comparison purposes. Over half of the general public (53%) who said they wanted to start a business also said they would act on the idea. The general public, however, gave more weight to the *very likely* (37%) than the *likely* (16%) response than did high school students, perhaps because members of the general public who were interested in starting a business were in a better position to take the entrepreneurial plunge given their education or life experiences. The general public most likely has a more nuanced understanding of acting upon a business idea. Whereas high school students might see the task of acting upon a business idea as a daunting one, the general public may view it simply as an addendum to their primary job. Nevertheless, there were about a quarter (23%) of this group interested in starting a business, who also stated that they are either *unlikely* (10%) or *not at all likely* (13%) to take this action.[8]

THE AGE FACTOR

As a final indicator of the great potential for entrepreneurship among youth, consider a question asked only of small business owners (Table 2.4). This group of entrepreneurs was asked the age when they first thought about starting or owning their own businesses. What is surprising is that these first thoughts occurred for many of them at a relatively young age. Almost two in ten (17%) expressed entrepreneurial interest when they were less than 20 years old. Another two in ten (20%) developed this idea when they were 20–24 years old. Almost three in ten (29%) thought about starting a business from 25 to 30 years old. What these results mean is that the first thought about entrepreneurship occurred for two-thirds (66%) of small business owners when they were young, in high school, or during their twenties. Only about one-third of them (32%) came to think about entrepreneurship for the first time when they were over 30 years old. The initial thoughts about being an entrepreneur enter the mind early in the lives of small business owners. These findings suggest it is worthwhile for education in entrepreneurship to begin at an early age and that it should continue throughout high school because these years can be an especially formative period in shaping the thinking of potential future entrepreneurs.

Table 2.4 Age When Thought of Starting Own Business[a]

| | Business Owners | | |
Response	Total (n=403)	Male (296)	Female (107)
	%	%	%
Less than 20 years old	17	18	16
20–24	20	23	14
25–30	29	30	28
Over 30 years old	32	28	41
Don't know/Refused	2	2	0

Note: [a]"How old were you when you first thought about starting or owning your own business?"

It is also the case that job experience serves as a significant precursor to thinking about entrepreneurship. The 25–30-year-old segment was the largest one that started thinking about entrepreneurship among the respondents who were 30 years old or less. This segment includes individuals who probably had completed their education and also had some job experience. In the context of working at a job, they may have identified an unfilled niche that would have market value and could be the key idea for starting their own business venture. Early experience in working for others may serve as a primary frame of reference for thinking about starting a new business and spark an enduring interest in becoming an entrepreneur.

The male and female responses of the business owners also are revealing about the timing of entrepreneurship. About the same percentages of males and females said they were less than 20 years old when they first began thinking about starting a business. This finding is important because it shows that the seeds of entrepreneurship are planted early in the minds of future business owners, regardless of their sex. Males, however, are more likely than females to cite their twenties as a formative period when they first started thinking about entrepreneurship. Females are more likely to say that they were 30 years old or older before they thought about starting a business, a response that probably has something to do with decisions about careers, marriage, and childbearing. Whatever the reason for the difference, the results clearly show that many female business owners did not start thinking about entrepreneurship until later in life. What the results also suggest is that more education about entrepreneurship in the early years may be a vehicle for equalizing some of the differences in first thinking about starting a business.

There is one final age-related factor that should be noted. Many business owners become interested in starting a business at a relatively young age and many also acted on these aspirations and started a business. One consequence of this early commitment to entrepreneurship is that these business owners often wind up creating more than just the initial business during their lifetimes. They have ample time over the course of their careers to act on their passion for entrepreneurship and create other businesses.

Among the small business owners surveyed, only one-third (33%) said that their current business was the *only* business they had either started or owned. The other two-thirds said they had started or owned one or more businesses. Almost a quarter (24%) had started one other business. Almost two in ten (17%) had started two other businesses. Over a quarter (26%) had started three or more other businesses.

These survey findings reveal that in most cases once someone starts a business the person is very likely to start other businesses. In other words, the entrepreneurial spirit is often not a one-time event but is more likely to be a mindset or attitude that spawns several businesses over time. From the perspective of the overall economy, more jobs and greater prosperity are likely results from the multiple ventures created by entrepreneurs.

REASONS OTHERS START BUSINESSES

The strong desire to start a business that was expressed by high school students, the general public, or business owners arises for many reasons, but several were viewed as more important than others (Table 2.5). This question focused on why the respondents thought *others* (as opposed to themselves) started ventures. Freedom and achievement are prime motivators for why other people start a business according to all three groups.

Almost all (89%) small business owners either *strongly agreed* or *agreed* that the reason people go into business was to be their own boss. The large majority of these small business owners also stated that the reason other people often become entrepreneurs was to use their skills and abilities (78%) and to build something for their family (73%). Of less importance as a motivating reason for entrepreneurship for these small business owners was the desire to earn lots of money (57%) or to overcome a challenge (45%).

Table 2.5 Reasons Other People Go into Business[a]

Reasons	SA	A	U	D	SD
A. To earn lots of money					
High school students (n=1010)	54%	24%	15%	4%	3%
General public (n=607)	49	20	22	5	4
Business owners (n=403)	38	19	29	11	3
B. To be their own boss					
High school students	52%	25%	16%	5%	2%
General public	75	14	7	3	2
Business owners	70	19	9	1	1
C. To use their skills and abilities					
High school students	37%	36%	19%	6%	2%
General public	53	25	15	5	2
Business owners	56	22	16	3	2
D. To build something for their family					
High school students	35%	33%	21%	8%	2%
General public	59	21	15	3	2
Business owners	51	22	21	6	2
E. To overcome a challenge					
High school students	19%	23%	37%	15%	6%
General public	26	23	29	13	8
Business owners	27	18	35	12	6

Note: [a]"Using a five-point scale, where 5 means you strongly agree and 1 means that you strongly disagree, do you think people go into business:"

The general public had about the same rank-order for reasons and indicated about the same degree of support for each reason as shown by the small business owners. The large majority of them also *strongly agreed* or *agreed* that the reason other people start businesses was to be their own boss (89%), build something for the family (80%), and use their skills and abilities (78%). Making lots of money was viewed as important (69%), but much less so than was the case with the other options.

By contrast, high school students gave their highest ranking to earning lots of money (78%) or being your own boss (77%) as the primary reasons why other people become entrepreneurs. This split opinion and the difference in the results for small business owners or the general public may stem from the thinking that others are more wealth- and acquisition-oriented than they are in their reasons for starting a business.[9]

REASONS *I* WANT TO START A BUSINESS

When an open-ended question was asked of the sample of high school students and the general public who stated that they were interested in starting their own businesses, the nature of the motivating reason changed (Table 2.6). The major reason for starting a new business, given by about half (45–48%) of those who were interested in starting a business, was the independence factor – being your own boss. Earning lots of money as a motivating reason was given significantly less often. Only about two in ten high school students (20%) or members of the general public (18%) supplied this answer as their reason for becoming an entrepreneur.[10]

The low rating that high school students gave to earning money as the prime motivation for them in starting a business may seem at odds with the greater importance they attached to this reason for entrepreneurship in others in the previous question (see Table 2.4). The responses are not contradictory, and unlikely just to be the result of differences in the definition of the two samples. High school students probably thought that earning lots of money was less important as a motivating reason *when they wanted to start a business*. They felt that it was much more important as a motivating reason *when others wanted to start a business*. Other studies found that high school students are service-oriented and not just seeking monetary rewards. Their thinking about starting a business seems to combine an entrepreneurial spirit with a social or community mindset that wants to help others and their communities.[11]

Table 2.6 Major Reason You Want to Start Own Business[a]

Response	High School Students (n=664)[b]	General Public (n=281)[b]	Business Owners (n=403)
To be my own boss	45%	48%	47%
To earn lots of money	20	18	9
To use my skills and abilities	11	9	20
To overcome a challenge	4	5	5
To build something for the family	3	6	9
To help the community/Provide jobs	3	4	–
To make a job	–	–	7
Other	4	7	6
No specific reason	6	2	0
Don't know/Refused	4	1	0

Notes:
[a]"What is the major reason why you might want to start a business for yourself?"
[b]For YES respondents on whether you'd want to start a business of your own.

Small business owners also were asked the question of why they wanted to start or own their current businesses. The overwhelming response, given by almost half (47%) of these small business owners, was to be in charge of their lives by being their own boss. It is amazing how entrenched the desire for autonomy is, especially given that most of these business owners had gone through the harrowing experience of starting their businesses. They had to learn how to manage the extensive risk and uncertainty of building the businesses. They had put in long hours of work and had often forgone vacations. The initial payoff from all this heartache and work can often be minimal for the business owner, and may only increase if the business becomes successful. Starting a business can be just as uncontrollable as working for another person, yet this desire for autonomy still ranks first by far among business owners. The other major reason given was to use their skills and abilities (20%). These two reasons account for two-thirds of all the open-ended responses. Earning a lot of money was a major motivating reason for less than one in ten (9%) and equal in importance to building something for the family.

One of the major reasons why small business owners wanted to be their own boss is because of a past job experience, which in many cases was a negative one. When the small business owners were asked for the first significant event or experience that prompted them to start or own their current business, half (50%) cited a job-related reason. The three major reasons given were a past job (12%), job dissatisfaction or burnout (15%), and losing a job (15%). Clearly, the desire for making your own job and being your own boss instead of taking an unfulfilling job offered by someone else or accepting the insecurity of employment in the job market was a major motivating reason for why these small business owners wanted to be entrepreneurs. There were also positive reasons given. Some business owners (17%) cited spotting a viable business idea or opportunity as a reason why they started their businesses.

Analysis of the open-ended responses by gender among high school students showed some differences in their personal perspectives on entrepreneurship (Table 2.7). Almost half (49%) of high school females thought the major reason they would start their own businesses would be to be their own boss. A plurality of males (42%) also thought this way, but a substantial percentage of males (26%) also thought the reason was to earn lots of money. Fewer females (13%) found this reason to be very compelling, and it was about the same percentage as those who said it was to use their skills and abilities (12%). This significant difference between males and females in the category "to earn lots of money" may suggest gender-biased notions of starting a business. Perhaps the traditional belief of the man as the significant breadwinner of the household accounts for some of this difference. The other reasons were supplied by less than one in ten females and males, and at about the same percentages.

Table 2.7 Major Reason for Wanting to Start Own Business[a]

Response	High School Students					
	Total (n=664)[b]	Male (325)[b]	Female (339)[b]	White (398)[b]	African American (176)[b]	Hispanic (142)[b]
	%	%	%	%	%	%
To be my own boss	45	42	49	47	46	34
To earn lots of money	20	26	13	19	19	26
To use my skills and abilities	11	9	12	11	9	10
To overcome a challenge	4	5	4	4	6	7
To build something for the family	3	4	2	3	5	4
To help the community/ Provide jobs	3	4	3	5	2	3
Other	4	4	4	3	5	5
No specific reason	6	4	8	6	5	7
Don't know/Refused	4	3	4	4	2	3

Notes:
[a]"What is the major reason why you might want to start a business for yourself?"
[b]For YES respondents to starting a business of your own (see Table 2.2).

Also worth noting are a few differences by race and ethnicity among high school students. Although being your own boss captured the highest percentage in each group, Hispanics were less likely than either whites or African Americans (34% versus 47% and 46%) to cite the independence factor. Hispanics were more likely than whites or African Americans (26% versus 19%) to list earning lots of money as a primary motivating reason for starting a business. This strongly suggests a different notion of business between Hispanics and the other groups. Perhaps starting a business for Hispanics is more of a collective effort. The other responses drew about one in ten or less responses from each group and there were few important differences.[12]

CHALLENGES AND OBSTACLES

Small business owners identified many challenges to starting a business, but some were thought to be more difficult than initially anticipated for people who start a business (Table 2.8). These responses are reported in ascending order. About half (54%) of small business owners thought that coming up with good ideas was more difficult. About six in ten indicated that either competing with other businesses (58%) or obtaining loans and financing (60%) were more difficult. About seven in ten either identified the problem of handling government regulation and red tape (71%) as an unexpected challenge or noted that it was developing sales (72%). About eight in ten (77%) thought the unanticipated challenge was controlling costs for the business.

Table 2.8 More Difficult Challenges in Starting a New Business[a]

Response	High School Students (n=1010)	General Public (n=607)	Business Owners (n=403)
Competing with other businesses	81%	79%	58%
Developing sales	76	78	72
Coming up with good ideas	75	61	54
Obtaining loans and financing	73	75	60
Controlling costs	71	81	77
Handling government regulation and red tape	59	71	71

Note: [a]"Which of the following challenges do you think prove to be more difficult than initially anticipated by people who start a new business?"

Roughly the same percentage of high school students (73%) as the general public (75%) responded that obtaining loans and financing was a more difficult challenge than expected, but these percentages were much higher than the percentage of small business owners (60%) who selected this option. Similarly, competing with other businesses was viewed as a more difficult challenge than expected by high school students (81%) and the general public (79%) than was the case among small business owners (58%). The one item on which high school students showed the least awareness was of the difficulties created for new businesses by government regulation and red tape.[13] Only about six in ten (59%) thought that this was more challenging compared with those in the general public (71%) or small business owners (71%).[14]

What is clear from surveying small business owners is that the obstacles to starting a business are many and varied, if the need for financial support to start the business is omitted from the questioning. Small business owners cited the following list of greatest obstacles to starting their current businesses: the demands to grow the business (16%), cash flow problems (11%), marketing concerns (11%), organization issues (10%), a willingness to take the risk (9%), dealing with employees and customers (8%), being able to handle government regulations (6%), young age or lack of experience (5%), a lack of education or skills (5%), and coming up with a good idea (2%). None of the items stand out as the most critical one. What these results suggest is that entrepreneurship education should be broad-based, both in terms of education and experience, so future entrepreneurs are best able to handle the many challenges of starting and running a business.

PREPARATION FOR ENTREPRENEURSHIP

This preparation for entrepreneurship can come from many sources (Table 2.9). About two-thirds of high school students (63%) indicated that school or college education would give them the most preparation. The general public and business owners, however, were significantly less likely to supply this answer (20% and 23%, respectively) probably because many of them had learned about the world of business outside of school or college. What was viewed as of about equal importance as education in preparation for entrepreneurship among small business owners was the job or business experience gained at working at another business (27%). Personal research through reading books or studying was also considered to be valuable (10%).[15]

These high school responses are especially valuable because they show that most youth who are interested in starting a business realize that they will gain the most preparation for entrepreneurship from their education. This result means that these youth are likely to be open and receptive to more entrepreneurship education at this age because they realize that it will be essential for fulfilling their aspirations to start a business. Many students, especially minorities, have little access to social resources that provide them with opportunities to learn entrepreneurial skills. By providing opportunities for entrepreneurship through a well-designed education program, schools can compensate for the lack of social capital among these youth. This would be just one way to level the playing field for potential entrepreneurs by decreasing some students' dependence on their own sparse social capital.

Table 2.9 Most Preparation for Starting Own Business[a]

Response	High School Students (n=664)[b]	General Public (n=281)[b]	Business Owners (n=403)
Education (school and college)	63%	20%	23%
Talking with other entrepreneurs	7	8	5
Working at business	6	13	27
Having financial backing	4	23	7
Life experiences	3	9	6
Personal research	1	8	10
Ability to spot an opportunity	1	5	1
Drive and hard work	–	2	7
Other	4	7	11
Don't know/Refused	11	7	4

Notes:
[a]"What do you think would give you the most preparation for starting your own business?"
[b]For YES respondents to starting a business of your own.

The lower percentages of the general public and business owners who cite education relative to that of youth should not be interpreted as the general public or business owners dismissing the value of education. The reason for their lower percentages is that as people age and mature, they find other sources of preparation for entrepreneurship, such as job or life experiences and networks that complement or substitute for education. Unlike the general public or business owners, high school students do not yet have extensive job or life experiences or networks upon which they rely, and their primary source of preparation will be education.

Even among business owners, there are important gender differences on the preparation issue. Female business owners (40%) show substantially more support for school or college education as the most important preparation for entrepreneurship than do male business owners (17%). Female business owners (8%) are more likely to cite the importance of talking with entrepreneurs than male business owners (4%). These percentages show the vital role that education or role models play in preparing women for entrepreneurship.

By contrast, male business owners (31%) are more likely to cite working at a business than are female business owners (15%). Male business owners (9%) also are more likely to note that financial backing is the most important preparation than do female business owners (1%). And a larger percentage of male business owners (9%) consider drive and hard work to be important preparation for entrepreneurship compared with female business owners (1%). These percentages indicate that male business owners give more credit to external business factors (job, finances, hard work) than to education or role models.

CONCLUSION

There is overwhelming interest in entrepreneurship among U.S. youth. It is an interest that cuts across gender, race, and ethnic lines. There is a significant reserve of entrepreneurial potential that is waiting to be fully realized in the United States. If ways can be found to encourage more youth to act on their entrepreneurial interest at some point over their lifetimes, such actions could significantly increase new business formation in the United States and improve the standards of living for all participants (entrepreneurs, employees, and their communities). Even those who do not start businesses may be able to use their entrepreneurial talents to enhance their careers and access. The economy also can benefit from increased entrepreneurial activity because it increases productivity, moderates inflation, and advances economic growth. At the same time, it provides opportunities to all individuals to improve their economic well-being and their communities.

NOTES

1. For the source of data reported in this paragraph see the chapter by Lowrey (2006) in *The Small Business Economy: A Report to the President* that was published by the Office of Advocacy, U.S. Small Business Administration, pp. 55–91 (www.sba.gov/advo/research/

sb_econ2006.pdf). It reports findings from the 2002 census of businesses and compares it with findings from the previous 1997 census.

2. Several reasons may explain this high level of interest in entrepreneurship among female youth. It may be that there are more examples of women who have succeeded in becoming successful entrepreneurs. There have also been changes in societal expectations and less discrimination against women in business. It should also be noted that this interest in entrepreneurship was not restricted to female youth, nor was it an attribute associated with youthful enthusiasm. In the general public survey, almost six in ten (58%) females expressed interest in starting a business over working for someone else if given the choice.

3. For the source of data see the *2002 Survey of Business Owners* (SBO) (U.S. Census Bureau 2006) (www.census.gov/csd/sbo/).

4. It is possible to speculate on the possible reasons for this high level of interest among African American and Hispanic youth. Becoming an entrepreneur may be especially appealing for minority youth because it may be a way of gaining access to greater pay, status, and control over life. They may come to realize at an early age that their economic opportunities might be increased if "they were the boss" rather than if they worked for someone else who will determine their pay and specify their path to economic opportunity.

5. One implication from this finding is that it suggests that entrepreneurship offers a potentially satisfying and flexible route for employment regardless of the particular initial circumstances of the aspiring entrepreneur. For example, immigrants who come to the United States, but who cannot speak English, may open a store that grows into a successful business. Additionally, many workers displaced by downturns in the economy or layoffs from corporations may turn this setback into an opportunity to start and build a successful business venture.

6. This gap seems to widen with age. Among a sample of youth and younger adults (ages 14–39), the gap moves toward almost two in ten (64% versus 47%). This gap is similar in size to that found in a survey of the general public (59% versus 42%).

7. The results from a 1999 survey of youth (ages 14–19) were similar. See Kourilsky and Walstad (2000), p. 16.

8. The responses of females and males also show a difference. Fewer females (49%) than males (57%) said they were very likely to act on an idea to start a business. The sample sizes for African Americans and Hispanics were quite small, so caution must be used in making comparisons. Over six in ten (62%) African American youth and over four in ten (41%) Hispanics said they were likely or very likely to start a business. Among white youth the response was about five in ten (52%)

saying they were very likely or likely to act on the idea to start a business.

9. The high school data were also analyzed for gender, race, and ethnic differences. There were minimal differences in the views of females and males about the reasons people go into business. There were, however, significant differences in view by race and ethnicity. African Americans and Hispanics were much more likely than whites to *strongly agree* with every proposition. For example, on the issue of "earn lots of money," 71% of African Americans and 61% of Hispanics strongly agree versus 49% for whites.

10. These results are similar to those found in prior years. For 1995 data, see Walstad and Kourilsky (1999), p. 21. For 1999 data, see Kourilsky and Walstad (2000), p. 23.

11. See Kourilsky and Walstad (2000), Chapter 1.

12. Not everyone wants to become an entrepreneur and it can be enlightening to find out why. Many reasons were given for *not* wanting to start a business among the minority (33%) of high school students who responded that way. The major reason for not wanting to be an entrepreneur was the lack of energy, time, skills, or ideas, stated by over one-third (37%). Of course, many of these concerns can be addressed through a proper education in entrepreneurship, an issue that will be addressed in Chapter 6. Other problems that concerned high school students were the problems of managing the business (11%), a satisfaction with their current situation (15%), or worries about the business risk (16%). There were few important differences between the groups based on gender, race, or ethnicity on this question.

   The portion of the general public who was not interested in entrepreneurship gave different weightings to the set of responses. Although they too cited a lack of energy, time, skills or ideas (24%) as a prime reason, it was not given the importance that high school students attached to this reason. What was of more concern to the general public were the age factor and the view that they were too old or too young for entrepreneurship, something that high school students rarely identified.

13. There were few differences between males and females on this question. There were also few differences among the responses of whites, African Americans, and Hispanics.

14. See Walstad and Kourilsky (1999), p. 45, for results with 1995 data.

15. See Kourilsky and Walstad (2000), p. 58, for results with a 1999 national sample. Education was rated most important, but by only 48%. The difference is probably because of the slight differences in samples. The current sample included high school youth (ages 14–18). The 1999 sample included youth (ages 14–19), some of whom were no longer in school.

3. Giving Back to the Community

In the previous chapter, the responses of high school students reveal substantial interest in starting their own businesses. Further probing conducted in this chapter finds a second significant and rather surprising message: two-thirds of these youth stated that they wanted to start a not-for-profit or charitable organization to help their community. This outcome is part of a marked tendency among young people to combine an entrepreneurial spirit with a Peace Corps mindset.[1]

These two responses require consideration of the underlying tensions and synergies between these parallel goals of many high school students. This chapter studies that issue by investigating the importance that youth attach to giving back to the community. In doing so, it answers several questions: Do youth think that businesses do in fact give back to their communities? If they do make such a contribution, what reasons do they perceive as motivating business owners to give back to the community? What role, if any, can social entrepreneurship play in resolving the apparent dissonance between students' parallel aspirations in the for-profit and not-for-profit environments? What new evidence is available to show that youth do in fact have both entrepreneurial interest and at the same time an orientation to starting non-profit ventures to do charitable work or improve the community?

INTEREST IN PHILANTHROPY

To start the investigation, high school students were asked a direct question: "Do you think you would want to start a not-for-profit or charitable organization to help your community?" (Table 3.1). Almost two-thirds (64%) of high school students responded said "Yes" to this philanthropic opportunity. Such a strong response from these youth was unexpected and almost equivalent to the percentage (65%) who said they wanted to start their own for-profit business or enterprise.

Table 3.1 Want to Start a Charitable Organization: High School[a]

Response	High School Students					
	Total (n=1010)	Male (444)	Female (566)	White (639)	African American (232)	Hispanic (205)
	%	%	%	%	%	%
Yes	64	57	71	61	77	69
No	35	42	28	38	23	29
Already started one	0	–	0	0	–	1
Don't know/Refused	1	1	1	1	1	2

Note: [a]"Do you think you would want to start a not-for-profit or charitable organization to help your community?"

These results suggest a pairing of potentially conflicting objectives in the minds of youth: starting a business venture, whose priorities are typically oriented toward such economic goals as identifying markets, creating and selling successful products for consumers, and generating revenues and profits, and starting a not-for-profit, whose priorities typically are oriented toward social goals such as charitable work, community betterment, or social reform.

The overall results for youth can be subdivided by demographic factors. Perhaps the most striking is that there are significant differences in the responses of males and females on this question. Over seven in ten (71%) females said they wanted to start a charitable organization compared with less than six in ten (57%) males. Although both sexes are greatly interested in philanthropic work, females show markedly stronger support for it.

This result appears consistent with extensive research on sex differences related to generosity, altruism, and empathetic tendencies. In surveys and experimental studies, females have been found to be more generous and more empathetic than men, and more likely than men to list altruism as one of their life goals.[2] In addition, women are more often employed in the caring and nurturing professions in the U.S. labor force. For example, most nurses, social workers, and teachers are women. Women are more likely than men to do volunteer work and participate in community activities.[3] There is also most likely a cultural or historical element for greater female support of charitable activity that may affect the thinking of female youth today. Throughout U.S. history, females traditionally have devoted their time to helping others through bearing and rearing children, working in the home, and volunteering, and thus were less often employed in the wage-earning or profit-making sectors of the economy.

There are also some important differences based on race. African American youth expressed the greatest desire to start a non-profit organization, with almost eight in ten (77%) stating that they wanted to start a non-profit to help their community. Only about six in ten (61%) white youth gave an affirmative response. The responses of Hispanic youth fell in between the two races with about seven in ten (69%) stating that they wanted to start a charitable organization.

The strong orientation of African American youth to create some kind of venture that helps their community may be a manifestation of what some scholars of the African American experience have called communalism. It refers to a cultural perspective in which "individuals view themselves as being inextricably linked with others in their social milieu."[4] It has been tied to a range of behaviors that include, among others, a tendency to be more cooperative and to be more concerned about family and ethnic group members. Given this perspective, it seems reasonable to suggest that the disproportionate desire of African American youth to start a "social enterprise" may be a byproduct of communalism.

OTHER PERSPECTIVES

The interview results from the general public and business owners show important, but somewhat less interest in wanting to start a non-profit venture (Table 3.2). Many individuals among the general public (45%) do have a desire to start some kind of charitable organization, but to a much smaller degree than do high school students. A likely reason for this difference was suggested in the previous chapter, and it is the age factor. The general public is a group that is substantially older. It is reasonable to expect that many of the older adults in the general public sample have family or financial obligations or commitments that would inhibit them from wanting to start a non-profit venture. They would be expected to be concerned first and foremost with meeting these obligations and only secondarily with aspiring to assist their community through a non-profit enterprise.

This age factor can be roughly investigated by splitting the general public sample into two age groups at the median age of 43. As noted in the previous chapter, those members of the general public who are 42 years old or less are in the prime age for entrepreneurship and also likely to be more interested in starting a non-profit venture. The results do show a substantial difference based on age. Over five in ten (51%) of those members of the general public who are 42 years old or less say they are interested in starting a non-profit compared with less than four in ten (39%) who are 43 years of age or older.

Table 3.2 Want to Start a Charitable Organization: All Groups[a]

Response	High School Students (n=1,010)	General Public (n=607)	Business Owners (n=403)
Yes	64%	45%	39%
No	35	51	57
Already started one	0	1	4
Don't know	1	2	1

Note: [a]"Do you think you would want to start a not-for-profit or charitable organization to help your community?"

Turning to the business sample, the data show that business owners are less likely (39%) than the other two groups to be interested in starting a non-profit. Part of the reason for this difference in response is that some business owners have already started a charitable organization or non-profit (4%). When combined with the percentage expressing interest in starting a charitable organization or non-profit, the total percentage (43%) is about the same as the interest expressed by the general public (45%).

The lower percentage of interest among business owners than high school students may be explained by the likelihood that many owners of small businesses are focusing primarily on building and expanding their businesses and ensuring their profitability. This work requires time and financial commitments that do not allow the possibility of taking on another major commitment such as starting a charitable organization or non-profit. Business owners also may be giving back to the community in other ways such as volunteering to serve in community organizations or by making charitable contributions.

Unlike the general public, owners of small businesses may show more interest in starting a non-profit as they get older because their businesses are established and they may have the financial resources to undertake such a venture. Partial support for this statement comes from splitting the business owners sample at the median age of 50 years old and examining the responses. Among those business owners who are 49 years of age or less, only 35% want to start a non-profit organization compared with 42% who are 50 years of age or older. Also, 5% of those 50 years of age or older have already started such an organization compared with only 3% who are less than 50 years old.[5]

RESPONSIBILITY TO THE COMMUNITY

The philanthropic focus now turns to their views about the social responsibility of business. One question (Table 3.3) delved specifically into the non-economic contributions of businesses to a community. Respondents were asked to rate, on a scale from one to five, where "5" is "very important" and "1" is "not at all important," how important it is for successful business owners or entrepreneurs to contribute something to the community *beyond providing jobs and paying taxes*. About half of all three groups gave the highest rating and stated it was "very important" for businesses to give back to the community. Of the three groups, the general public most often (57%) said giving back was very important, followed by high school students (49%) and business owners (48%).

Table 3.3 Importance of a Community Contribution: All Groups[a]

Response	High School Students (n=1,010)	General Public (n=607)	Business Owners (n=403)
5 Very important	49%	57%	48%
4	31	24	23
3	15	11	22
2	3	3	4
1 Not at all important	2	4	3
Don't know/Refused	1	2	1

Note: [a]"Using a five-point scale, where 5 is very important, and 1 is not at all important, how important do you think it is for successful business owners or entrepreneurs to contribute something to the community beyond providing jobs or paying taxes?"

Not only did about half of the three groups respond that it was very important for successful business owners to contribute something to their communities, the distribution of responses for all three groups was similar across all the other response categories. For example, at the other extreme, about the same small percentages of high school students (2%), the general public (4%), and business owners (3%) stated that community contributions were *not at all important* for successful business owners to make. Thus, the similarity in the results across the three groups suggests that there is a common cultural value that pervades the population and crosses age and ownership boundaries. Most Americans share the belief that successful business owners should contribute something to the community beyond providing jobs and paying taxes.[6]

When business owners were separated into subgroups based on the number of employees, the responses vary in predictable ways. Business owners who owned firms with more employees were more likely to think that community contributions were very important. Owners of firms with 21–49 employees were more likely to view philanthropy as very important compared with owners of firms with 1–9 employees (61% versus 46%). Owners of firms with 10–19 employees fell in between the two percentages (57%), but were closer in views to owners of firms with the most employees.

The sizable difference in support for philanthropy that separates the owners of firms with the fewest and greatest number of employees is probably attributable to financial constraints and business stability. Firms with a few employees typically have less cash flow and are less economically secure than firms with more employees. Firms with more employees also are likely to be more established and there may be greater expectations for them to contribute to a community because they have more capacity to share part of their business success by making a charitable contribution.

The business owners' results can also be subdivided by gender. Female business owners were highly more likely to state that it was very important for successful business owners to give back to the community than were male business owners (59% versus 44%). This result was not surprising given the prior discussion of differences in generosity and altruism between men and women, and the fact that women give more than men to charitable causes.[7]

IMPORTANCE OF PHILANTHROPY

Although there are few differences among the three main groups about the philanthropic responsibility of businesses, a closer look at differences within the high school sample reveals several sharp contrasts (Table 3.4). When high school students are divided into subgroups by race and ethnicity, an important difference emerges between African American youth and white youth, or between African American youth and Hispanic youth, in their attitudes toward the importance of community contributions. A larger percentage of African American students (65%) thought that giving back to the community was *very important* for entrepreneurs to do than did white students (44%) or did Hispanic students (48%).[8] Perhaps the strong orientation to giving back can be better understood by examining the data from the opposite end of the scale. In this case, the data show that only 35% of African American students thought that business-based philanthropy was *anything less than very important* compared with 55% of whites or 50% of Hispanics.

Table 3.4 Importance of a Community Contribution: High School[a]

Response	Total (n=1010)	Male (444)	Female (566)	White (639)	African American (232)	Hispanic (205)
	%	%	%	%	%	%
5 Very important	49	47	50	44	65	48
4	30	31	31	33	19	29
3	15	15	14	16	11	18
2	3	3	3	4	2	2
1 Not at all important	2	2	1	2	1	1
Don't know/Refused	1	2	1	1	2	2

Note: [a]"Using a five-point scale, where 5 is very important, and 1 is not at all important, how important do you think it is for successful business owners or entrepreneurs to contribute something to the community beyond providing jobs or paying taxes?"

The results from African American students to the two survey questions reinforce each other. African American high school students wanted to start their own non-profit businesses more often than did whites or Hispanics, and they thought that it was very important for entrepreneurs to contribute something to the community more so than the other groups. This outcome provides further evidence that a "communalist" mindset prevails among African American teenagers. Such a mindset is likely to result in for-profit ventures among young African Americans that are more community-oriented and philanthropic, and thereby may add more value to society than would be the case with a for-profit venture that just provided jobs or paid taxes.

REASONS TO CONTRIBUTE

Possible reasons a business owner might contribute to a community *beyond* providing jobs or paying taxes can appear to be both "self-interested" and "altruistic." A list of five such reasons was generated, two that were more altruistic (help the community; believe in voluntary giving) and three that were more self-interested (promote their business; want people to remember their names; and it is tax deductible). Youth believed that the major reason business owners made contributions to the community stems largely from self-interested motives (Table 3.5). The option selected by three-fourths (75%) of youth was to "promote their business." Half (50%) of youth cited "remember their names" as a major reason, and almost half (46%) of youth stated "it is tax deductible" as a major motivator.

Table 3.5 Major Reasons for Contributing to Community[a]

Response	High School Students (n=1,010)	General Public (n=607)	Business Owners (n=403)
They want to promote their business	75%	85%	75%
They want to help the community	52	58	73
They want people to remember their name	50	66	60
It is tax deductible	46	60	38
They personally believe in voluntary giving	35	40	57

Note: [a]"For each possible reason a business owner or entrepreneur might have for contributing to the community beyond providing jobs or paying taxes, do you think it would be a major reason, a minor reason, or not a reason at all?"

These results may suggest that youth are somewhat skeptical about the motives of business owners or entrepreneurs for giving back to the community. That perception is perhaps dominant, but it should also be noted that there was some support for altruistic motives even if the frequencies of selection were not as high as those for the more self-interested motives. A little over half (52%) of youth believed that successful business owners or entrepreneurs contributed to the community because they "want to help the community" and over three in ten (35%) perceived that business owners contribute to the community because they "personally believe in voluntary giving."[9]

The general sentiment can be shown by averaging the two self-interested responses and the three altruistic responses. In this case, 57% of youth responses would be self-interested and 43% would be altruistic. These overall results indicate that there has been a reversal from 1996 when the altruistic responses to this question averaged 64% and self-interested responses averaged 54%.[10]

This shift over time may have occurred because of the preponderance of high-visibility corporate scandals in recent years such as those involving Enron, World Com, or Global Crossings. It may also reflect a more skeptical opinion about the motives of businesses for giving to the community, regardless of whether they are large or small businesses. This opinion may have arisen because of adverse effects on domestic employment such as the economic developments of downsizing, offshoring and outsourcing of jobs. This conclusion, however, should not be taken to the extreme of thinking that youth are anti-business or cynical about business motives. The current data show that high school students attribute a mixture of motives for giving, some purely economic and more dominant, but others also purely social and philanthropic.

The interview protocol also allowed analysis of what youth thought were "minor reasons" for businesses to contribute to a community. The outcome from this other direction reinforced the above findings and was intuitively consistent. For example, only 22% of youth thought that promoting their business was only a minor reason, so it would be expected that a larger percentage (75% in this case) might think it was a major reason. Similarly, 50% of youth thought that a belief in voluntary giving was a minor reason, so it would be expected that a lower percentage (35%) would think it was a major reason.

Compared with high school students, the general public is more skeptical and cynical about business. The responses with the most support as major reasons why business owners or entrepreneurs contribute to a community are to promote themselves (85%), get people to remember their name (66%), and receive a tax deduction (60%). All three are economic factors. The two philanthropic factors, wanting to help the community (58%) or a personal belief in voluntary giving (40%), receive less support. The pattern of their responses indicates that the general public, more so than high school students, thinks that economic considerations are more important than social considerations when business owners make their decisions about philanthropic contributions.

A sample of adults was also asked this question in the 1996 survey that included high school students. The 1996 results showed a much stronger support for the social considerations because 72% said a major reason was to help the community and 56% said a major reason was because of a belief in voluntary giving. The percentage citing the social factor of helping the community as a major reason was also essentially the same as the 73% citing the economic factor of business promotion as a major reason. The likely reasons for the difference in results from 1996 to 2002 were the ones discussed for high school students. It may be that more skeptical or anti-business attitudes developed over that period because of the bad publicity from corporate scandals or adverse and highly publicized developments affecting the domestic workforce.[11]

Business owners' views of their own motives were similar to high school students with several key exceptions. First, the responses of business owners showed a more balanced profile between what were considered to be the main economic and social considerations. Their top two reasons for contributing to the community in ways other than by providing jobs or paying taxes were also self-promotion and wanting to help the community, the same top ones stated by high school students. Most business owners, however, gave the two reasons about the same high rating, with 73% saying that helping the community was a major reason and 75% saying that promoting a business was a major reason. Second, there were sharp differences in views about a belief in voluntary giving. Only 35% of high school students thought that it was a major reason for giving, but a much larger percentage of business owners (57%) indicated that this belief was a major reason.

On reflection, the above results showing a mix of economic and philanthropic motives for giving are not surprising as business owners, on average, do probably give, for a variety of reasons. What is perhaps more surprising is that the thinking of business owners is not more dominated by economic factors. Most businesses are started with economic goals in mind such as creating a product or service, finding and developing a market, acquiring financial and other resources, and initiating and sustaining an operating business venture. At the early stage, most businesses owners must work hard at simply surviving, and in turn this survivor experience may shape later thinking about the reasons to give contributions. Unless a business is organized around non-profit or social goals at the outset, it is the rare business owner who has significant financial resources available to invest in philanthropic or community development. It is also the rare business owner who can step back from the pressure to achieve or maintain a profitable business, and ask how it can contribute in significant ways to the community, unless social considerations are included as part of the business plan.

CONTRIBUTIONS TO THE COMMUNITY

The previous question asked *why* business owners contributed to the community. The next questions focus on *what* they contribute. An open-ended question asked people to state what they thought business owners or entrepreneurs contributed to the community where they were located (Table 3.6). The responses then were divided primarily into two common factors used in the previous discussion: economic and philanthropic. Some respondents also gave some other responses which were coded as "other," or they gave a "nothing" or "don't know" response.

Almost half (48%) of high school students listed an economic factor that business owners contributed to the community. These factors included such responses as providing jobs and contributing through money, goods, services, or paying taxes. Another 17% of youth named philanthropic contributions such as giving money to charities or establishing charities. Almost one-third of youth, however, either said that business owners contributed "nothing" to their communities (4%) or they "don't know" (28%).

Table 3.6 Contributions Business Owners Make to the Community[a]

Response	High School Students (n=1,010)	General Public (n=607)	Business Owners (n=403)
A. Economic factors	75%	85%	75%
B. Philanthropic factors	52	58	73
C. Other	50	66	60
D. Nothing	46	60	38
E. Don't know	35	40	57

Note: [a]"What, if anything, do you think business owners or entrepreneurs contribute to the community where they are located?"

What is encouraging is that a significant fraction of teenagers perceived at some level when business owners or entrepreneurs help create jobs, enrich markets, provide useful products and services, and pay taxes, they are making an important economic contribution to a community. Other youth also recognized the philanthropic contribution businesses make to a community. Taken together, almost two-thirds of youth were aware of one or the other major type of contribution businesses made to communities. What is disconcerting about the responses, but also expected, was the large fraction of youth who do not recognize any contribution made to the community by business owners. About one-third of high school students were unable to identify a community contribution made by business owners when they gave a "nothing" or "don't know" reply to the question.[12]

Of the two-thirds who had something to say at all about how businesses contribute to their communities, less than two in ten of teenagers perceived business owners making philanthropic contributions. The component factors of that percentage primarily included giving to or establishing charities and doing public service work. These numbers indicate that even as teenagers affirm the importance of businesses giving back to the community, those who express an opinion have a low perception (by frequency of identification) of the philanthropic contributions made by businesses.

The low perception probably reflects a lack of knowledge among teenagers of business owners' contributions to society. It could also serve as a disincentive for today's youth to engage in entrepreneurship as they go forward with their careers because they may not want to be identified with a group that is not perceived as altruistic. If such is the case, it is unfortunate that this disincentive is manifesting itself at a time when both social concerns (in areas such as schooling and health care) and economic concerns (in areas such as global competition) are on the rise.

There were differences between the way young people and business owners responded to the questions concerning how business owners and entrepreneurs contribute to the communities where they are located. Predictably, only a few (7%) business owners either refused to answer the question or claimed not to know how they and others like them add social value to their communities. More commonly, business owners responded that they contributed to their communities in economic terms by providing jobs (42%), contributing to the economy (24%), and paying taxes (4%). In total, seven in ten (70%) business owners named economic factors as their community contributions. Some business owners, however, did identify the philanthropic contribution, but it was at a lower level (12%) than that reported for high school students (17%).

Interestingly, when compared both to teenagers and to business owners, the general public had a more positive view of the philanthropic contributions that businesses make to communities. Over two in ten (23%) of the general public identified a philanthropic contribution of businesses. Almost six in ten (57%) of the general public also cited the economic contribution that businesses make to communities. Only about two in ten gave either a "nothing" response (6%) or did not know (13%). Clearly the general public is more aware of contributions that businesses make, either economic or philanthropic, probably because many of them have resided in their communities for a long time and see those contributions.[13]

DUELING ASPIRATIONS

The results presented in the last chapter and this one showed great interest in youth in starting a for-profit venture and also in starting a non-profit or charitable organization. About *two-thirds* of youth want to start a business of their own (Table 2.2). About the same proportion of youth wants to start a charitable organization (Table 3.1). A cross-tabulation of the responses from the two questions was conducted to investigate the degree of overlap between the entrepreneurial aspirations and the philanthropic aspirations among youth.

These results are remarkable and show that a great majority of youth do hold two such aspirations. Of the 65% of youth who stated that they wanted to start a business of their own, 71% also said that they wanted to start a non-profit or charitable organization (Table 3.7). The issue can also be considered from the opposite perspective. Among the 64% of youth who stated that they wanted to start a non-profit or charitable organization, 72% also stated they wanted to start a business of their own. In either case there is a substantial overlap in thinking and it is important.

Table 3.7 Want to Start Charitable Organization by Yes to Entrepreneurship[a]

| Response | High School Students | | | | | |
	Total (n=664)[b]	Male (325)[b]	Female (339)[b]	White (398)[b]	African American (176)[b]	Hispanic (142)[b]
	%	%	%	%	%	%
Yes	71	61	83	68	82	72
No	28	37	16	31	18	26
Other	1	2	1	1	–	2

Notes:
[a]"Do you think you would want to start a not-for-profit or charitable organization to help your community?"
[b]For YES respondents on whether you'd want to start a business of your own (see Table 2.2).

For the sake of parsimony, these latter findings are not reported in table form and are not discussed further. They do, however, indicate that similar results will be found regardless of whether the analysis is conducted starting from the perspective of interest in entrepreneurship and then exploring interest in creating a philanthropic venture, or whether the analysis is conducted starting from the perspective of the desire to create a philanthropic venture and then seeing if there is also interest in creating a business venture.

From the perspective of known interest in entrepreneurship, the results show that there is strong proclivity on the part of most youth to also have a philanthropic mindset. These youth aspire to become business owners so they can take control of their lives, build successful businesses, and perhaps accumulate wealth. But these youth are not totally self-interested or driven by pecuniary motives. At the same time, they aspire to make a valuable contribution to society and the communities in which they live. These philanthropic or social aspirations certainly are a significant part of the thinking of this generation of entrepreneurial youth.[14]

The analysis also supports previous discussion about male–female differences. It was noted that various studies have found that women are more likely than men to give more to charity and to volunteer more in the community. It was not surprising, therefore, to find that a much greater percentage of female youth were interested in starting a non-profit or charitable organization than were male youth (71% versus 57%), regardless of whether they wanted to start a business (Table 3.1). When the data are cross-tabulated to account for interest in starting a business, the affirmative response rises and the percentage-point spread between male and female youth widens. Holding entrepreneurial interest constant, 83% of females stated they were also interested in starting a non-profit or charitable organization compared with 61% of males. Among the great majority of females who are interested in entrepreneurship there is also a similar interest in making a philanthropic contribution.

The contrast in opinions was also found for whites and African Americans. The previous discussion had noted that other studies have found a strong orientation among African Americans to help their community. The previous results (Table 3.1) show this general sentiment among African American youth compared with white youth in regard to starting a non-profit or charitable organization (77% versus 61% favored starting such a venture). When the sample is restricted to those youth who are interested in starting a business, the level of interest increases and the gap between white and African American youth widens somewhat: 82% of African American youth also say they want to start a philanthropic venture compared with only 68% of white youth.

The findings for Hispanic youth fall in between those for whites and African Americans but show a similar level of changes. For all Hispanic youth, 69% stated they were interested in starting a philanthropic venture. Among those Hispanic youth who are interested in becoming entrepreneurs, 72% were also interested in starting a philanthropic venture. Many Hispanic youth also want to undertake both types of ventures.

Further evidence on the strong relationship between entrepreneurial and philanthropic interest can be found in the general public data. Less than half (45%) of the general public stated they were interested in starting a non-profit or charitable organization (Table 3.1). This result suggests that this interest is not particularly great among the general public. The reasons that were previously discussed suggest that age, family or work circumstances, or financial resources may play a role in keeping this percentage relatively low for the general public. When the analysis, however, focuses on the sub-sample of the general public who stated they were interested in starting a business, there is a substantial change in the percentage. Almost two-thirds (65%) of the general public who are interested in starting a business (n=281) were also interested in starting a philanthropic venture. The dueling aspirations to become an entrepreneur and at the same time help the community or society are present among the general public as well as youth.

RESOLUTION?

A final question to be asked is how the dueling aspirations will be handled and resolved. Some youth may think that the aspirations of wanting to start a business and wanting to start a non-profit or philanthropic organization are achievable simultaneously and see no contradiction. Thus, they may anticipate initiating a business venture that may or may not be successful depending on many variables such as their knowledge, preparedness, and passion – in addition to quality of product, vagaries of the market, "being in the right place at the right time," and so on. Furthermore, even if they are able to keep the business viable, there may not be enough surplus resources left to be able to also start a charitable organization or even to donate as much as they would want to such an organization. These youth, however, are being unrealistic and simply dreaming.

More often teenagers may understand the contradiction between starting a for-profit venture and initiating a non-profit or charitable organization, but not knowing how to resolve the issue, they do nothing. They are "frozen in the headlights" so to speak. Ultimately, the teenagers who experience this dilemma can select several paths. They can forgo starting a not-for-profit venture to initiate a profit-making enterprise or visa versa. Alternatively, these young people can decide that one or the other of these aspirations is of secondary importance and pursuing it can wait until later. It is also possible for high school students who experience this dilemma to pursue another strategy that might help them achieve both goals that would involve providing them with access to knowledge about "social entrepreneurship" as a career alternative. A full discussion of that valuable resolution strategy, and its rationale and implications, is beyond the scope of this chapter and can be found in the last chapter of the book.[15]

CONCLUSION

This chapter compared the attitudes and opinions of high school students with those of the general public and small business owners regarding the responsibilities of businesses to their community and the importance of "giving back." The primary finding was that about equal numbers of youth aspired to initiate for-profit businesses as hoped to found non-profit organizations in the future. This current generation of teenagers includes many potential entrepreneurs who also have a community orientation.

When asked about the importance of contributions from business owners to the community, high school students – like members of the general public and business owners – thought in substantial numbers that it was very important for successful business owners to "give back" to a community. Apparently, this generation had a vision of business owners or entrepreneurs contributing to their communities in ways that did not necessarily stop at paying taxes and providing jobs.

When asked, however, whether and how business owners currently contributed to their communities, high school students showed a lack of knowledge. They thought that business owners were motivated primarily by economic benefits and only secondarily by "altruistic" concerns, which was supported in general by the responses of business owners themselves. Nevertheless, high school students underestimated the importance business owners attributed to voluntary giving. They also could name few non-economic ways in which businesses typically contributed to their communities. Negative publicity generated by illegal activity of large corporations in recent years may have combined with this lack of knowledge to leave young people with a negative impression of the social responsibility of businesses.

Many high school students want to start for-profit businesses and they also want to start a non-profit or charitable organization. How can sense be made of these apparently dueling aspirations? Although some teenagers might believe in the "pipedream" that both goals can be achievable simultaneously, in reality that possibility is highly unlikely. Other teenagers might be paralyzed by the dilemma. They know it will be difficult to achieve both of their goals at the same time, but don't know what to do about it, and therefore do nothing. A third possibility is that some of these youth will want to participate in social entrepreneurship, a topic to be addressed in the final chapter of the book.

NOTES

1. This theme was initially explored in our previous study (Kourilsky and Walstad 2000). Such youth have been labeled "Generation-E" and a "distinguishing feature of this new generation, besides their age, is that entrepreneurial attitudes are often joined with the idea that successful entrepreneurs have a responsibility to improve the community in which they live" (p. 5). This chapter provides further support for that theme and those findings using this more current data.
2. Eckel and Grossman (1998) found that "women, on average, donate twice as much as men to their anonymous partners." Not only do women display more empathy, they also are more likely than men to list altruism as one of their life goals. The Higher Education Research Institute at the University of California (Los Angeles) persistently finds in its annual survey of the attitudes and preferences of college freshmen that approximately two-thirds of women say "helping others who are in difficulty" is an essential or very important life objective, compared to only half of the men (Pryor et al. 2006). In a survey on altruism in

America, the National Opinion Research Center at the University of Chicago (NORC) found that women proved to be more empathetic than men: they were more likely to feel pity for others and to describe themselves as soft-hearted. Females also professed more altruistic values. Just like the college women in the UCLA study, more women than men in the NORC survey strongly agreed with statements such as "personally assisting people in trouble is very important to me."

3. A 2005 study by the U.S. Department of Labor reported that 30% of women performed volunteer work compared to 24% of men.

4. Boykin, Jagers, Ellison, and Albury (1997), p. 410.

5. These results are only suggestive of what might be found because subdividing the total sample of 403 business owners by age and studying only several categories of response to a question ("yes" or "already started one") reduces the sample size for comparative purposes to 172 business owners.

6. This belief may be part of a sense of the social contract that is historically associated with the American character (Acs and Phillips 2002).

7. See Rooney, Mesch, et al. (2005). Controlling for marital status and effects of survey methodologies, this study demonstrated both single and married women gave more than single and married men. See also Kaplan and Hayes (1993), Council of Economic Advisors (2000), Giving USA Foundation's annual report (researched and written at the Center on Philanthropy at Indiana University, 2005), and Taylor and Shaw-Hardy (2006).

8. These differences appear to hold over time. A similar question was asked in a 1995 survey of youth (ages 14–19), but there were just three categories for response to the question (very important, somewhat important, and not at all important). In that survey, eight in ten (80%) African Americans said it was very important compared with only six in ten of whites (61%) (see Walstad and Kourilsky 1998). The response that it was very important was given by only six in ten Hispanics (60%).

9. There were no noteworthy ethnic differences among youth. There were also only slight differences by gender. The largest difference was on one of the altruistic items. More females than males (56% versus 47%) stated that "They want to help the community" as a major reason for contributing to the community.

10. For a discussion of the 1996 results for this item, see Walstad and Kourilsky (1999), pp. 94–96.

11. For the 1996 results, see Walstad and Kourilsky (1999), pp. 94–96. Another reason for the difference over time aside from the one given in the text may be due to the composition of the samples. The adult sample in 1996 samples was younger (18–39 years of age) compared with the full general public sample (18–65+ years of age). This slight sampling

difference, however, is not likely to be the full explanation for the significant shift and it is more likely due to the forces cited in the text. The shift over time for the general public was also found with high school students, and in that case the two samples were directly comparable.

12. These percentages, however, also represent an improvement over the findings from a 1996 survey of youth. In that study, only 25% identified an economic factor and only 13% identified a philanthropic factor. The predominant responses were either "don't know" (47%) or "nothing" (9%) (see Walstad and Kourilsky 1999, p. 91).

13. When analysis was conducted of the differences within each of the three groups (high school students, business owners, and the general public), there were no remarkable gender, racial, or ethnic differences that stood out from the interview results for this question.

14. This theme has been explored in a previous work (Kourilsky and Walstad 2000). Such youth have been labeled "Generation-E" and a "distinguishing feature of this new generation, besides their age, is that entrepreneurial attitudes are often joined with the idea that successful entrepreneurs have a responsibility to improve the community in which they live" (p. 5).

15. Youth's desires both to start a for-profit and to start a not-for-profit venture is a case of concurrent cognitions. This phenomenon in which two concurrent cognitions are discrepant is called cognitive dissonance (Festinger 1957). When most people are faced with two cognitions that are inconsistent, a typical response is to do *nothing*. This dissonance may be reduced in three ways: (1) incorporate a new cognition to help reduce the dissonance; (2) eliminate one of the discrepant cognitions; or (3) alter the importance or impact of one of the cognitions. A discussion of how a new cognition (social entrepreneurship) can be used to resolve this problem will be explained in the last chapter.

4. Entrepreneurial Knowledge

High school students who hope to join the prosperity they see at the high ends of the wage and income scales require knowledge and skills to leverage their entrepreneurial aspirations, but face a barrier in their lack of economic knowledge, business management know-how and entrepreneurial skills. This chapter documents the unmet needs of high school students for more entrepreneurial knowledge of this kind.

To assess to what degree the lack of entrepreneurial knowledge erected a barrier to income, careers, and social mobility for many youth, a set of knowledge questions was included in this survey to resemble a short, multiple-choice test because the practical constraints of surveying the three groups eliminated the possibility of administering a long test. This short test included six items that were considered to be a representative sample of a broad range of possible business management and basic economics questions regularly included in the entrepreneurship content domain.[1] The questions were worded so that most teenagers could easily comprehend them. They had been reviewed by content experts in entrepreneurship and also checked by survey specialists at The Gallup Organization for any survey bias. Most important, they had been used as reliable and valid indicators of entrepreneurial knowledge in previous national surveys of youth.[2]

As a preview of the results, it should not be a surprise to find that many teenagers lacked knowledge in subjects related to entrepreneurial activity. Previous studies have found that many youth are woefully ignorant about many basic concepts and ideas related to entrepreneurship, business, and economics.[3] One reason for this situation is that many youth receive little or no formal training in entrepreneurship, business, or economics in their education. This topic will be investigated in a later chapter in the book, and it will discuss the type of education youth need to receive for meeting that demand and to correct the inequity in the distribution of entrepreneurial knowledge. This chapter, however, focuses on the test results and what they reveal about the entrepreneurial understanding of youth.

KNOWLEDGE SCORES

The "entrepreneurship exam" portion of our interview was designed to assess high school students on their knowledge of topics that business owners generally understand well because they are concepts and skills integral to the practice of starting and operating a business. Thus, the six items that comprised this part of the interview included questions about the definition of the term "entrepreneur," the role of small business in jobs creation, the necessities of business survival, the definition of a "franchise," the law of supply and demand, and the purposes of profits.

As expected, business owners had the highest score on the test, with almost eight in ten (79%) business owners supplying a correct response (Table 4.1). This score is high, but it might be expected to be higher for this knowledgeable and experienced group. There are several reasons why this outcome is not the case. First, the sample of business owners was diverse. Not all business owners should be expected to have a complete knowledge of economic and management topics. Some owners had more extensive education, including undergraduate or graduate study, while others have not.[4] Perhaps some business owners inherited a family business, or became entrepreneurs out of necessity, and thus had to gain knowledge and skills through their experience in starting a venture. Second, mistakes and lapses in memory were to be expected even among business owners because they, like the other two respondent groups in this study, had not prepared for the types of questions on this short test.

Table 4.1 Entrepreneurial Knowledge Questions

Score	High School Students (n=1,010)	General Public (n=607)	Business Owners (n=403)
Description of entrepreneur	74%	85%	90%
Small business and job creation	31	55	70
Business survival	47	66	82
Example of franchise	63	85	95
Supply and demand	64	71	85
Purpose of profits	34	41	51
Mean	**52%**	**67%**	**79%**

The score for the business owners represents a baseline for comparison with the other two groups. Overall, high school students, on average, could answer correctly only about half the questions (52%). The general public scored higher and gave correct answers to about two-thirds (67%) of the questions. These results suggest that there were substantial gaps in the knowledge of high school students and the general public on questions of knowledge and understanding of entrepreneurship and business.

This score distribution – with high school students scoring the lowest and business owners demonstrating the most entrepreneurial knowledge – was to be expected. High school students were not expected to do as well as business owners or members of the general public because they likely had little or no business education or experience. As the more detailed analysis that follows shows, teenagers knew the answers to some questions better than they knew the answers to others. This difference in response pattern reveals the particulars of knowledge gaps among high school students that are useful for educators or mentors who seek to provide young people with the education necessary to become entrepreneurs or entrepreneurial in their thinking.

ENTREPRENEUR

The first question on the test was a basic definition: "Which of the following best describes an entrepreneur?" The possible answers were "a person who starts a business," "a manager of a large corporation," or "a government official running a regulatory agency." Most respondents in all three groups gave correct answers to this question, so the definition of "entrepreneur" in the simplest sense of the term appears to be widely understood. Nine in ten (90%) business owners correctly answered this question. Over eight in ten (85%) of the general public gave a correct answer. Over seven in ten (74%) high school students knew the answer. This term appears to be widely understood and is in common use among all three segments of the population.

The high level of correct responses should not mask another concern. Most high school students knew the correct meaning of the term "entrepreneur," but about a quarter did not, either because they gave incorrect responses or did not know. Fifteen percent thought an entrepreneur was the manager of a large corporation and 7% thought an entrepreneur was a government official. Three percent did not know. Many of these students probably had no exposure to the concept of entrepreneurship and business during their high school education.

The high school results can be studied by gender, race, and ethnicity (Table 4.2). There were only very minor differences based on sex or race. Hispanics, however, had the highest rate of misunderstanding of this term relative to whites or African Americans. These results suggest that for this minority group there may be a lack of exposure to core concepts.

Table 4.2 Description of an Entrepreneur[a]

	High School Students					
Response	Total (n=1010)	Male (444)	Female (566)	White (639)	African American (232)	Hispanic (205)
	%	%	%	%	%	%
A person who starts a business	74	76	73	75	74	63
A manager of a large corporation	15	16	15	15	16	18
A government official running a regulatory agency	7	6	9	7	8	14
Don't know/Refused	3	3	3	3	2	5

Note: [a]"Which of the following best describes an entrepreneur?"

JOBS CREATION

The second question asked about the contributions various types of businesses make to jobs creation: "Over the past ten years, which of the following groups has created the most jobs in the economy?" Since most entrepreneurs, especially first-time entrepreneurs, are small business owners, the intent of this question was to reveal what young people knew about one of the important roles of small business in the economy.

The correct answer to this question was that small businesses had created the most jobs in the U.S. economy over the previous ten years.[5] The great majority (70%) of business owners knew the correct answer to this question. By contrast, only about three in ten (31%) high school students correctly answered this question (Table 4.3). This result means that about seven in ten high school students have some misconception about the role of small businesses in jobs creation. Almost half of all teenagers reported that they thought large businesses created the most jobs. Perhaps surprisingly, almost two in ten thought the Federal government created the most jobs.

African American students gave a correct answer more often than did whites or Hispanics. About the same proportion of African American students erroneously attributed more jobs creation to large businesses, but this incorrect response (40%) was lower than the ones for either white or Hispanic youth. The data indicate that African American youth were more likely to know about, or perhaps had more experience with, the jobs creation by small businesses than did the other groups of high school students.

Table 4.3 *Who Created the Most Jobs?*[a]

| Response | High School Students | | | | | |
	Total (n=1010)	Male (444)	Female (566)	White (639)	African American (232)	Hispanic (205)
	%	%	%	%	%	%
Small businesses	31	31	30	30	38	27
Large businesses	49	49	49	51	40	46
The Federal government	19	19	19	18	22	26
Don't know/Refused	3	3	3	3	2	5

Note: [a]"Over the last ten years, which of the following groups has created the most new jobs in the economy?"

The general public was better informed about small businesses creating the most jobs in the economy, but not as well informed as business owners. A little over half of the respondents who were members of the general public (55%) gave the correct answer, but about three in ten agreed with high school students that it was large corporations that created the most jobs. A smaller, but still substantial proportion (13%), of the general public believed the Federal government created the most jobs. In comparison to high school students, then, the general public more often knew the correct answer to this question concerning jobs creation, and they less often answered incorrectly by reporting that the Federal government drove jobs creation, but in about the same proportion as high school students they reported that large businesses had employed the most people.

The common misperception that large companies with many employees employ the most people is perhaps understandable given their size, well-known and advertised names, and the attention they attract from the media. Small firms get neglected or overlooked as a consequence even though there are many more small businesses than large businesses in the U.S. economy. In fact, small firms account for 99.7% of all employer firms and they employ half of all employees in the private sector.[6] Each small business, however, employs a small number of employees compared to each large firm such as a Wal-Mart, Ford, or IBM. Nevertheless, the sheer number of small firms means that as a group they are the largest force for the creation of jobs in the economy.[7]

Since three in ten business owners answered the question about jobs creation incorrectly, it was worthwhile to explore the differences between better-informed and less well-informed entrepreneurs. The interview design allowed differentiation of business owners by sex and by their business's number of employees. To the question of what groups created the most jobs in the previous ten years, more men (73%) than women (62%) correctly answered.[8] Also, among business owners who employed 20–49 employees (the largest possible number of employees in the interview protocol), almost eight in ten (79%) knew the correct answer to this question compared with about seven in ten (69%) who correctly answered among owners with firms that employed 1–9 employees. This finding may indicate simply that those with more employees naturally have first-hand experience with jobs creation. These respondents belong to the group of business owners who drive the most jobs in our economy.

BUSINESS SURVIVAL

The next question asked, "Which factor is most important for business survival?" This question measured whether teenagers understood the value of several business management factors including cash flow, stock, corporate organization in the form of a board of directors, and depreciation. The correct answer to this question was that cash flow is the most important factor for a company's survival. The value of a company's common stock – which was the second choice in this item – is clearly not important to a company's survival in all cases simply because not all companies issue and trade stock publicly. In fact, the great majority of small businesses are privately held, often by one proprietor or one family. Likewise, having a board of directors is not a key factor in business survival; many successful businesses are much too small to have a board. Having a low depreciation rate is merely a cost factor and has no direct bearing on a firm's survival. On the other hand, without adequate cash flow, a business cannot continue to produce goods or services, which requires purchasing supplies and raw materials and paying for labor or other production costs on a day-to-day basis.

The responses to this question showed that less than half (47%) of the high school students understood the importance of cash flow to a business's survival (Table 4.4). Almost a quarter (24%) of these teenagers incorrectly reported that the value of a company's stock was the most important factor for success. Almost two in ten (17%) said that having a board of directors was the key element and another one in ten answered that a low depreciation rate was of paramount importance. It is likely that the respondents who answered this way were simply guessing. No substantial differences existed between males and females. In terms of race and ethnicity, Hispanics supplied a correct answer only 37% of the time, which was lower than the percentage for whites (50%) and African Americans (44%).

Table 4.4 Most Important Factor in Business Survival[a]

	High School Students					
Response	Total (n=1010)	Male (444)	Female (566)	White (639)	African American (232)	Hispanic (205)
	%	%	%	%	%	%
The company's cash flow	47	49	46	50	44	37
The value of the company's common stock	24	49	23	21	28	31
Having a board of directors	17	25	18	15	20	20
Having a low depreciation rate	10	16	10	11	7	12
Some/Combination/All	1	9	1	0	0	–
Don't know/Refused	1	1	2	1	0	1

Note: [a]"Which one of the following factors is the most important for business survival?"

If this question about factors contributing to business survival can be taken as a sample question partially representing management knowledge, then this area appeared to be a particularly weak, although not the weakest, part of the entrepreneurial knowledge of teenagers. Whereas only half of all high school students answered this item correctly, two-thirds of the general public knew the answer. Only 15% of the general public thought that a company's stock was the most important factor. The disparity in correct responses between high school students and the general public is an interesting phenomenon because it suggests, as previously surmised, that although high school students were not well versed in business management issues, members of the general public somehow, in the years since they had attended high school, had acquired additional knowledge, perhaps through business-related experience, most likely through working. As expected, the great majority (82%) of business owners knew the crucial role cash flow plays in business survival because many in this group had first-hand experience with this situation.

FRANCHISE

The fourth question asked participants to select a correct example of a franchise. This question did not ask for an open-ended definition of a franchise, nor did it even ask respondents to choose one from several multiple-choice definitions. Instead, interviewers simply asked respondents to identify which well-known company was organized as a franchise. The choices were a McDonald's restaurant, the IBM Corporation, or a General Motors-Buick plant. The purpose of asking the question was to make a determination about a common business organization type and whether it was widely familiar or relatively unknown. The correct answer, of course, was a McDonald's restaurant.

It was expected that many high school students and members of the general public, and certainly business owners, would correctly answer this question, with the percentages correct increasing in that order. The fact that so many members of the general public, and probably even more high school students, were well acquainted with a McDonald's restaurant as consumers was one reason to expect most people would correctly answer this question. The results met the expectation for high levels of correct responses and rank-order by group. Over six in ten (63%) high school students, over eight in ten (85%) of the general public, and over nine in ten (95%) business owners selected the correct answer.[9]

The response for youth, at over six in ten giving a correct answer, appears to be positive at first glance relative to the other questions on the test (Table 4.5). Unfortunately, over two in ten (22%) high school students thought that it was the IBM corporation and more than one in ten (13%) thought it was a General Motors-Buick plant. Clearly, a sizable portion of high school students were just guessing when it came to choosing an example of a franchise. There were no major differences in the responses of males and females. African American and Hispanic students were less likely to get this item correct than were whites (57% or 51% versus 65%), and they were more likely to select the incorrect choice of IBM (25% and 34% versus 21%).

Table 4.5 Example of a Franchise[a]

	High School Students					
Response	**Total** (n=1010)	**Male** (444)	**Female** (566)	**White** (639)	**African American** (232)	**Hispanic** (205)
	%	%	%	%	%	%
A McDonald's restaurant	63	64	62	65	57	51
The IBM corporation	22	23	21	21	25	34
A General Motor-Buick plant	13	12	13	12	17	12
Some/Combination/All	0	–	0	0	–	–
Don't know/Refused	2	1	4	1	0	4

Note: [a]"Which one of these three businesses is the best example of a franchise?"

PRICES

The last two questions on the entrepreneurship test overlapped with economics. These items were designed to indicate youth's grasp of the basic economic principles that drive an entrepreneurial economy. Specifically, it was important to know if participants correctly understood the concepts of supply and demand, prices, and profits. Toward this end, one question focused on how prices are set and another was concerned with the purpose of profits. Most high school students receive some instruction in economics, so it was expected that a substantial number would grasp these basic concepts, which also are important for business management and venture initiation.[10]

The fifth question on the test asked how the prices of most products in a competitive market, like the United States, are determined (Table 4.6). This question was intended to provide an indication of young people's knowledge of markets. The correct answer to the question was supply and demand. In recent years, government only rarely sets prices. When government has intervened to set establish prices, such markets are no longer competitive. Therefore, a respondent who answered that the government sets prices revealed his or her ignorance of the basic concept of a competitive market. A respondent who answered, alternatively, that the Consumer Price Index (CPI) sets prices was probably just guessing since the CPI is simply a measure of the general level of prices. Those respondents who replied that the Federal Reserve's monetary policy sets prices expressed their misunderstanding of the Federal Reserve, because the policies of that institution are designed to target and change the Federal funds rate, and not to determine the prices of goods and services.

As expected, most business owners (85%) knew the correct answer to this question. Even a large majority (70%) of the general public supplied a correct answer. Nearly two-thirds (64%) of high school students gave a correct answer question to this question. Although a conclusion to be drawn from these results is that overall most high school youth understand how prices are set, there is still significant room for improvement when the high school data are examined in greater detail (Table 4.6). Perhaps the disturbing part of this is that over one-third (36%) of high school students do not understand how prices are determined, which is fundamental to understanding competitive markets. For example, about one in seven youth said prices were determined by government and another one in seven youth said prices were determined by the CPI. African American and Hispanic youth also were less likely than white youth (55% versus 66%) to supply a correct answer and more likely than white youth (20% versus 13%) to think that government sets prices in a competitive market.

Table 4.6 Determination of Prices[a]

Response	High School Students					
	Total (n=1010)	Male (444)	Female (566)	White (639)	African American (232)	Hispanic (205)
	%	%	%	%	%	%
Supply and demand for products	64	65	62	66	55	54
Local, state or Federal government	15	14	15	13	20	20
The Consumer Price Index	14	13	14	14	14	16
Monetary policy of the Federal Reserve	6	6	6	5	8	7
Don't know/Refused	2	2	2	2	2	3

Note: [a]"To the best of your knowledge, the prices of most products in a competitive market, like the United States, are determined by the:"

PROFITS

The sixth and final question asked high school students about the purpose of profits in a market economy and gave three possible options: first, profits reward businesses for producing what consumers want to buy; second, profits pay for the wages and salaries of workers; and third, profits transfer income to the wealthy. Some respondents may have agreed with all of the possible responses or some combination of them.

The correct answer to the question was the first choice: profits reward businesses for producing what consumers are willing to buy. As with many of the other questions, the incorrect options were chosen with care. Each incorrect option was designed to reveal a bias or misconception about business management, markets, government regulation, or economics. In the case of this question, the intention was to determine whether respondents knew the basic purpose of profits. If respondents answered that wages and salaries are paid out of profits, they would reveal their own misconceptions about financial matters, confusing profits with revenue. The question was worded in such a way that anyone without fundamental knowledge or elementary exposure to economics or business management subjects would probably guess incorrectly, and thus a high rate of incorrect answers was expected.

As anticipated, almost two-thirds (65%) of all high school students answered this question incorrectly (Table 4.7). Fifty percent of the responses were that profits pay for wages and salaries of workers. This result implies that teenagers confused profit with gross revenue, which in turn suggests they do not understand the primary reward that accrues to business owners in exchange for taking risk and expending effort in their ventures. Another 15% believed that profit transfers income to the wealthy, which may indicate that some teenagers equate profit with unbalanced distribution of wealth in society and feel that profits accrue to others and are unlikely to be something these teenagers themselves ever acquire.

Table 4.7 Purpose of Profits[a]

	High School Students					
					African	
	Total	**Male**	**Female**	**White**	**American**	**Hispanic**
Response	(n=1010)	(444)	(566)	(639)	(232)	(205)
	%	%	%	%	%	%
Reward businesses for producing what consumers want	34	32	36	32	42	33
Pay for the wages and salaries of workers	50	50	50	52	42	47
Transfer income to the wealthy	15	16	13	14	16	18
Some/combination/all	0	1	0	1	–	–
Don't know/Refused	2	2	1	2	–	2

Note: [a]"Which of the following do you think is the basic purpose of profits in our market economy?"

Although not reported in a table, a slim majority (41%) of the general public answered this question about profits correctly by indicating that the basic purpose of profits is to reward businesses for producing what consumers want, but almost as many (36%) answered, like high school students, that profits pay for salaries and wages. Another 17% thought that profits transferred income to the wealthy. If the incorrect responses are combined, they total 56%, indicating they did not understand profit.

More business owners (51%) than the general public (41%) or high school students (34%) knew the basic purpose of profits, so the expected rank-order in correct responses by group is preserved even with this difficult item. This outcome, however, is not impressive and shows that almost half (47%) of them gave an incorrect answer. This result speaks to the difficulty of this item and suggests that the term "profits" is widely misunderstood and confused with revenue even among business owners. Nevertheless, high school students are less well informed than the other two groups.

A further breakdown of the high school data shows a key difference by race and ethnicity. African American students are more likely than white students (42% versus 32%) to give a correct response. There is about the same amount of difference between African American students and Hispanic students (42% versus 33%). African American students are also less likely than white students (42% versus 52%) to think incorrectly that the purpose of profits is simply to pay for wages and salaries of workers.

AWARENESS OF ENTREPRENEURIAL KNOWLEDGE

The low overall score on the entrepreneurship test and the number of incorrect responses on individual items in this portion of the survey indicate that high school students may have substantial deficiencies in their economics and business management knowledge and entrepreneurial skills. As a further check of these findings, another question was asked on the survey to investigate whether the low scores on the knowledge items were consistent with a self-assessment of entrepreneurial knowledge. Did young people also believe they lacked the requisite knowledge to achieve their entrepreneurial aspirations, or did they consider themselves well educated and prepared to start their own ventures?

To answer this question, the following question was asked: "Using a five-point scale, where '5' is 'excellent,' and '1' is 'very poor,' how would you describe your knowledge and understanding of starting and managing a business?" The results gave insights into the respondents' level of knowledge in terms of some basic economics and business concepts. The results from the self-assessment would permit a rough comparison to be made between the level of entrepreneurial knowledge as measured by the test item and how highly teenagers self-rated their level of entrepreneurial knowledge.

The results show that the self-rating of high school students on their entrepreneurial knowledge was consistent with the low scores on the entrepreneurship test (Table 4.8). Over three-fourths (77%) of high school students gave themselves the three lowest ratings: fair (47%); poor (22%), or very poor (8%). The remaining fourth (23%) gave themselves the two highest ratings: good (18%) or excellent (5%). Most youth rated themselves at the middle or bottom of the scale suggesting they lack confidence in their knowledge of starting and managing a business. Only a quarter rated their knowledge as good or excellent, which suggests that few young people had confidence in their knowledge and skills related to entrepreneurship.

Table 4.8 Knowledge of Starting and Managing a Business[a]

Score	High School Students (n=1,010)	General Public (n=607)	Business Owners (n=403)
5 Excellent	5%	15%	13%
4	18	19	16
3	47	34	34
2	22	16	21
1 Very poor	8	15	16

Note: [a]For high school students and the general public the question was: "Using a five-point scale, where 5 is excellent, and 1 is very poor, how would you describe your knowledge and understanding of starting and managing a business?" For business owners, the question was the same except at the end of the question the following phase was added: "at the time you started your current business."

On the test items, the jobs creation item was the question high school students most often answered incorrectly, but even 31% of the high school respondents reported the correct answer to it. It should not be surprising, therefore, that about a quarter of high school students also would say in reply to the self-assessment item that they are well prepared in these important knowledge areas. The results show that high school students appear to be both accurate and realistic in self-assessment of their entrepreneurial readiness, at least as it is related to knowledge of important economics and business management concepts.

The general public gave responses that were similar to those of high school students. Almost two-thirds (65%) of the general public thought their knowledge and understanding of starting and managing a business was only fair (34%), poor (16%), or very poor (15%). In contrast to high school students, however, about one-third (34%) of the general public rated itself as good or excellent. The difference between high school students and the general public, then, represents a jump from one-fourth to one-third. More often, the general public leaned toward the higher end of the scale. Since members of the general public responded correctly to items on the entrepreneurship test more often than did high school students, the general public's higher self-rating seems to be realistic.

There appears to be a confidence difference in the response of the general public and high school students. For the general public the lowest percentage correct on any of the test items was 41% on the item related to the purpose of profits. The general public may be more knowledgeable about economic and business management-related topics than is indicated by its self-assessment. The general public may be less confident about their entrepreneurial knowledge and skills, perhaps because their experience has taught them that the skills and areas of expertise needed for successful ventures are larger and more varied than what could be captured in the entrepreneurship test.

Business owners also responded to the question in which they were asked to rate their own level of business-related knowledge, except that their question was worded slightly differently. Business owners were asked to rate their knowledge and understanding of starting and managing a business *at the time they started their current business*. Obviously in retrospect, these small business owners realized that they had a lot to learn and that they were not as educated or well prepared at the time they started their current businesses as they were after some years of operating those businesses.

Not surprisingly, then, the responses of business owners were about the same as those of the general public. About three of ten business owners (29%) reported their knowledge and understanding of starting and managing a business to be good (16%) or excellent (13%) at the time they started their current businesses. About seven of ten (71%) of business owners reported their knowledge and understanding of starting and managing a business at the time they started their current businesses to be fair (34%), poor (21%), or very poor (16%).

Interestingly, compared to both high school students and the general public, a higher percentage (37%) of owners of small businesses rated themselves at the very bottom of the scale in terms of business initiation and management knowledge. This difference may be attributable to business owners remembering how unprepared for starting and operating a business they actually were and also from knowing now all the depth of knowledge and skills that are needed to start a successful business. It also reflects the lack of education that they may have received for starting a business, whether that education was provided in the schools or colleges and universities.

Among high school students, self-rating of entrepreneurial knowledge varied by race (Table 4.9). Most students rated their own knowledge as fair, poor, or very poor in the same way, regardless of the composition of the group: all students (77%); males (78%); females (79%); white youth (79%); and Hispanic youth (77%). African American students, however, had a less negative assessment of their own entrepreneurial knowledge and understanding (66% said it was fair, poor, or very poor). From the opposite perspective, African American youth said they were more confident in their entrepreneurial knowledge and skills. Whereas less than a quarter (23%) of all high school students rated their entrepreneurial preparation as either good or excellent, one-third (34%) of African American students gave themselves these ratings.

Table 4.9 Knowledge of Starting and Managing a Business by Characteristic[a]

| Response | High School Students | | | | | |
	Total (n=1010)	Male (444)	Female (566)	White (639)	African American (232)	Hispanic (205)
	%	%	%	%	%	%
5 Excellent	5	4	5	3	11	5
4	18	20	16	18	23	19
3	47	46	47	48	43	44
2	22	22	23	23	14	20
1 Very poor	8	8	9	8	9	13
Don't know/Refused	0	–	0	0	1	–

Note: [a]"Using a five-point scale, where 5 is excellent, and 1 is very poor, how would you describe your knowledge and understanding of starting and managing a business?"

The higher self-rating of entrepreneurial knowledge among African American students was not reflected in their scores on the entrepreneurship test items. The average percentage correct on all test questions for African American students (52%) was the same as it was for all students (52%) and for whites (53%). These results suggest African American students are more confident in their preparation to be business owners than was indicated by their knowledge scores.

Results from other survey items (Tables 2.2 and 2.3) showed that African American youth have a greater interest in becoming their own bosses than do other students. This higher level of confidence may reflect a greater interest in and greater intent to start a business. One concern, however, with this mindset is that if this group of students is less prepared than they think they are, or that they need to be, then the survival of their future businesses may be impeded by their lack of economic knowledge and business management skills. Although this higher level of confidence is encouraging, it may be a risk factor unless it is matched with an entrepreneurship education that lifts the actual knowledge and understanding to its perceived level.

CONCLUSION

The entrepreneurship test and the self-rating permitted study of whether a lack of knowledge about entrepreneurship, economics, and management, areas vital to the successful realization of entrepreneurial dreams, were significant barriers for young people. The conclusion is inescapably that ignorance stands in the way of the aspirations of many high school students to achieve success, increase their income and wealth, and become more socially mobile. These young people are aware of their own lack of knowledge and deficiencies: they don't know enough about starting and managing a business and they *know* they don't know. This observation, combined with the strong interest among today's high school students in starting their own ventures and being their own bosses, amounts to a strong demand among young people to have more entrepreneurial knowledge.

Not only did the study findings expose an area of important need among youth, the questioning of respondents on their knowledge of the role of small businesses in jobs creation, the factors important to business survival, how prices are determined, and the role of profits, as well as important definitions like "franchise" and "entrepreneur," reveal a detailed picture of where high school students have some awareness and where they need additional instruction and experience.

The results show that many high school students are familiar with common terms like "franchise" and "entrepreneur," but many do not know much about the composition of the economy. What kind of firm creates the most jobs, for example? Their knowledge of management practices is slightly better, but still lacking. They need to know the components of business survival such as the importance of cash flow and the role of market capitalization and depreciation of assets in assessing a business's value in order to judge the viability of their own businesses as well as others. Teenagers were aware of how prices are set and understood something about the concept of supply and demand, probably reflecting that economics is taught in high schools, but they didn't understand well the purpose of profits or the difference between profits and revenues, which is indicative of a lack of exposure to real-world contexts and perspectives in their education.

The demand for more entrepreneurship education exists among high school students in the United States. The scope of this demand is indicated by the fact that high school students can correctly answer only three out of six test items on entrepreneurship and that three-fourths of high school students rate their entrepreneurial knowledge no better than fair. The situation can also be examined from the other side. About a quarter of high school students rate their knowledge of starting and managing a business to be good or excellent and, on average, about the same percentage knew the correct answers to the entrepreneurship exam test. Clearly, some teenagers are acquiring this entrepreneurial knowledge, but not enough are gaining the knowledge they need to achieve entrepreneurial success.

NOTES

1. Textbooks and curriculum materials provide examples of the entrepreneurship content domain. See Kent (1990), Kourilsky, Allen, Bocage, and Waters (1995), Kuratko and Hodgetts (1998), Lambing and Kuehl (1997), or Kourilsky (1999). The questions were worded so that most teenagers could easily comprehend them, they were reviewed by content experts, had been used in previous studies (Walstad and Kourilsky 1999), and were reviewed and edited by The Gallup Organization professionals to eliminate potential bias-related errors.

2. See Walstad and Kourilsky (1999), Chapter 4.

3. Walstad and Kourilsky (1999) report findings from a 1995 Gallup survey of using many of the same test items that will be used for this chapter. Kourilsky and Walstad (2000) use a different set of items to assess entrepreneurial knowledge and understanding. See also Walstad and Rebeck (2001) for findings on economics questions administered to high school students.

4. Further analysis of the business owners data indicates that education does contribute to score differences. The mean score on the six questions for the 213 business owners who were college graduates was 5.07 (0.92 standard deviation) or 85% correct. The mean score for the 188 business owners who were not college graduates was 4.35 (1.27 standard deviation) or 73% correct.

5. The following statement on the issue of jobs creation comes from the U.S. Small Business Administration: "Over the past decade, small business net job creation fluctuated between 60 and 80 percent. In the most recent year with data (2003), employer firms with fewer than 500 employees created 1,990,326 net new jobs, whereas large firms with 500 or more employees shed 994,667 net jobs." For a more complete look at employment dynamics by firm size from 1989 to 2003, see www.sba.gov/advo/research/data.html#us. Of course, employment is only one aspect of the major contributions that small businesses make to the economy. For a discussion of the multiple contributions of small business, see *The Small Business Economy: A Report to the President* (December, 2006): Washington, DC: Office of Advocacy, U.S. Small Business Administration.

6. Data reported by the Office of Advocacy, U.S. Small Business Administration in response to frequently asked questions. See http://app1.sba.gov/faqs/.

7. For research on small business and jobs creation, see Birch (1987), Haltiwanger and Krizan (1999), and Acs and Armington (2004).

8. Previous research showed deficiencies in entrepreneurial knowledge among teenage and young adult females (Kourilsky and Walstad 2005).

For a worldwide overview of female entrepreneurial activity including attitudes and educational profiles, see Minniti, Allen, and Langowitz (2005).

9. The characteristic of this multiple-choice question may have increased the percentage correct. This question had only three options compared with other questions that had four options, making it easier for a respondent to guess the correct answer.

10. For data and a discussion of course taking in economics, see Walstad and Rebeck (2000) or National Council on Economic Education (2005).

5. Markets and Government

Entrepreneurial knowledge and business skills are not the only areas that need more development among high school students who hope one day to achieve economic success and autonomy. Young people who anticipate becoming entrepreneurs must also acquire a broad-based and multifaceted perspective about economic issues that might be called the "ownership mindset." Do teenagers who aspire to start their own ventures already possess opinions and attitudes concerning public policy on economic issues that they would most likely find themselves exercising once they become their own bosses? Or, was this ownership mindset one area where high school students needed more development?

This chapter investigates how well high school students understand and adopt interests that correspond to the perspectives of business owners on matters of public policy. To gain insight into this matter, questions were included on the survey that asked business owners for their outlook on a number of economic issues related to prices, regulation, taxation, and the appropriate role for government in markets. Teenagers also were surveyed on the same issues so that their attitudes and opinions could be compared with business owners. The extent to which the attitudes and opinions of teenagers diverged from those of small business owners would be an indicator of whether teenagers had developed an ownership mentality regarding government and markets. Members of the general public were also surveyed on the issues to provide a further contrast for the other two groups.

It should be remembered in reading this chapter that unlike questions on the survey that sought to measure knowledge of economics and business management, questions that ask opinions about the optimal relationship between government and markets have no right or wrong answers. There are only answers that are more or less consistent with entrepreneurial aspirations and the experience of business owners. The questions in this case are being used to gauge the predominant opinions or attitudes of business owners and make comparisons with those of youth or the general public.

77

THE OWNERSHIP MINDSET

Successful entrepreneurs know and exercise a certain outlook or worldview that helps them to achieve prosperity. This mindset encompasses a wide range of mentalities broadly studied in entrepreneurship literature. Researchers list a number of mental qualities as characteristic of successful entrepreneurs including the following: "divergent thinking," which enables individuals to recognize extraordinary opportunities in what others see as ordinary problems; vision, which provides would-be entrepreneurs with a comprehensive idea of a future venture and an ability to communicate that venture to others; the willingness to take risks; and the ability to marshal people and resources to produce and market a service or good. None of these mentalities is an ingrained personality trait, though some young people may possess these habits of mind in greater quantities than others. Rather, entrepreneurial mentalities are an area for development that should be of concern to any quality education program that seeks to teach youth about entrepreneurship.[1]

In addition to these mental qualities of the successful entrepreneur, business owners also need to exercise an ownership mindset in relation to public policy. An ownership mentality entails viewing questions of public policy in terms of how they are likely to affect a business venture. Once an entrepreneur has taken the risk involved in initiating a venture and is committed to seeing that venture succeed, he or she generally adopts a clear view of how the government should function to support, rather than obstruct, entrepreneurial activities. For example, business owners typically view the issues of government regulation with a certain wariness that is not necessarily shared by the public at large. Business owners also tend to complain loudly about their tax burden. Of perhaps the most pertinent interest, they think of competitive markets as imperative to their success in providing a good or service that meets the needs of society. For an entrepreneur with an ownership mentality, any kind of market manipulation that distorts competition is anathema, whether it is by the government or by a market player with too much power.

Of course, economic policies are enacted that go against the interests of small business owners. The examples are many and they include minimum wage laws, rent controls, price controls, product rationing, regulatory policies and actions, and selective taxes on particular goods and services. In many cases, such laws are passed or government actions are taken because there are other economic interests or goals that are given more weight in the public discussion such as concerns about economic equality or economic security instead of economic efficiency. The debate on what policies are best suited to advance various economic and social goals often involve balancing the interests of business owners and with those of other groups in society and determining whether the goals can be accomplished without distorting the rationing function of the competitive market. In such debates, owners of small businesses, as one large and influential group, can be expected legitimately to pursue their own interests to let markets operate with minimal interference from government laws and restrictions.

SUPPLY AND PRICES

The first two items in the series of questions that assessed the ownership mindset of teenagers explored the issue of price setting and price controls by presenting interviewees with two different scenarios: one involving a supply shortage that resulted in higher producer costs and increased prices, and the other entailing high demand leading to higher prices. Price increases are obviously unpopular among consumers, who generally like to think they are getting a bargain or a low price. Previous research conducted with youth and the general public showed that many in each group think like consumers when they see a price increase and are often quick to conclude that price manipulation has occurred.[2] In the extreme case, they can suspect that corporations are seeking an unfair advantage by "gouging" helpless customers. This tendency is particularly strong when the good or service that has become more expensive is a vital one like energy, telecommunications, health care, housing, or transportation. When there are sharp and sustained increases in the price of gasoline, for example, the public and some elected officials clamor for price controls or some kind of government intervention to reduce the price. In these cases, a sizable proportion of the public supports government action to control prices and does not trust the market to set prices and allocate resources.

To gauge the support among the groups for the idea of government price controls, a hypothetical situation was presented: "If a shortage of lumber increased the cost of building houses, do you think the government should prohibit construction companies from raising prices on new houses?" Respondents had two options from which to choose: "yes, prohibit" and "no, do not prohibit." This question was relevant to the issue of entrepreneurship because many construction companies are small businesses started by entrepreneurs. The item also was designed to present young people with a scenario for price increases that might result from forces outside a business's control and that could not be attributed easily to price manipulation.

From an economics perspective, however, several arguments can be made against a policy of controlling prices in the housing market. First, when the cost of raw materials increases – in this hypothetical case the raw material is lumber – perhaps due to an external factor like weather, fire, a labor action, or raised shipping costs, construction companies likely would seek to recoup their increased costs in order to pay their bills and continue to build houses. To stay in business, these construction companies probably need to pass their increased costs on to the consumer. If the government prohibited these companies from recovering their costs, many would no longer be able to continue producing houses without damaging their businesses' solvency or their ability to meet market demand. From the perspective of the entrepreneur who is trying to survive in a competitive market, therefore, government caps on the ability of a company to raise its prices would be undesirable. High school students, however, might not approach a problem like this from an ownership mindset, even if they understood that supply and demand determine prices in competitive markets.

The good news is that over six in ten (61%) high school students said "no," the government should not prohibit construction companies from passing their increased costs on to customers (Table 5.1). The majority of high school students apparently recognize the value of letting markets set prices instead of having the government intervene, at least in this hypothetical case involving home construction.

Table 5.1 Government Should Prohibit Price Increases[a]

Response	High School Students (n=1,010)	General Public (n=607)	Business Owners (n=403)
Yes, prohibit	38%	34%	16%
No, do not prohibit	61	63	80
Don't know/Refused	1	3	4

Note: [a]"If a shortage of lumber increased the cost of building houses, do you think the government should prohibit construction companies from raising prices on new houses?"

The bad news is that almost four in ten (38%) high school students said "yes," the government should prohibit construction companies from raising prices. These students apparently believed businesses should absorb rising production costs and not seek to recover those costs in their sales. Whether this opinion represents a lack of knowledge on the part of teenagers, or whether it reflects a critical belief among some of them that all businesses are out to gouge the consumer or that government should intervene in the profit-making abilities of businesses, is uncertain. In any case, it clearly indicates the lack of an ownership mindset among this sizable minority of high school students.[3]

The general public answered this question in similar percentages as high school students. Over six in ten (63%) of the general public said the company should be permitted to raise prices when faced with a shortage that increased costs, thus suggesting that a majority of the general public see problems with government intervention to set prices in this case. By contrast, over three in ten (34%) said government should prohibit a construction business from raising prices when the cost of its raw materials increased, thus indicating that a sizable minority of the general public wanted to control prices and restrict business freedom.

Business owners, on the other hand, answered with a resounding "no," government should not prohibit businesses from passing on increased production costs. Eight in ten (80%) business owners answered in the negative – a substantial majority. Only a small percentage (16%) of business owners answered "yes." The response from this group may reflect the fact that some business owners are thinking more like consumers rather than producers because in this case they are not supplying this product. It is in the interest of most consumers to see lower prices instead of higher prices.

The results from this question were surprising. Most respondents from each of the three groups did not think the government should prevent businesses from raising prices when faced with increased raw material costs. Even high school students, the knowledgeable and educated group who were interviewed, thought markets should set prices in this hypothetical case. What was still unknown was whether this evidence of an ownership mindset was manifested in the responses to other survey items.

DEMAND AND PRICES

A second question was asked to test whether anti-price control views of the majority of teenagers held in other economic circumstances, or whether it was particular to a situation in which reduction in the supply of a resource forced producers to increase prices. Thus, a survey question needed to be asked that approached the issue of price setting from a *demand* rather than a supply perspective. The results from the previous question showed that most high school students agreed that higher production costs could legitimately result in higher consumer prices. The next question probed whether they also thought that an increase in demand should permit businesses to charge more for their goods or services.

The second hypothetical question was the following: "Suppose a bicycle manufacturer raises the price of bikes because the demand for them has increased even though the cost of producing bikes has not increased. Do you think the manufacturer should be allowed to raise prices?" The extent to which teenagers answered this question in the negative would suggest that they were not thinking like future business owners, that they did not understand how supply and demand worked to produce price equilibrium and that, instead, they were deferring to their sense of "fairness" as consumers.

Raising prices as a result of increased demand is a part of everyday economic life. It costs more to fly during peak travel times. Energy prices go up in the summer when air conditioners are running all day. Telephone rates are higher during business hours. Stock prices increase as the trading day progresses if more people are buying, and they decrease as traders sell off shares. And popular products have prices that bear little relation to what it costs to produce them. Still, when manufacturers or retailers raise prices in response to increased demand, they expose themselves to accusations of "gouging," or taking advantage of the consumer. Public attitudes are such that producers must not be seen to be exacting the maximum price for a product. For this reason, relatively few respondents were expected to state that they would allow the bicycle manufacturer to raise prices.

The original expectations appear to be met. About six in ten (61%) high school students replied "no," the manufacturer should not be allowed to raise prices if demand for bicycles increased (see Table 5.2). In fact, the percentage who opposed the price increase in the demand case was about the same as the percentage who opposed government intervention to control prices in the supply case. Apparently, for most high school students, supply constrictions that raised producer prices were legitimate causes of price increases, but if a price hike resulted because more people were willing and able to buy the product, then the legitimacy of the price increase was suspect.

Table 5.2 Manufacturer Should Be Allowed to Raise Prices: All Groups[a]

Response	High School Students (n=1,010)	General Public (n=607)	Business Owners (n=403)
Yes, allowed to	39%	47%	69%
No, not allowed to	61	52	29
Don't know/Refused	0	1	2

Note: [a]"Suppose a bicycle manufacturer raises the price of bikes because the demand for them has increased even though the cost of producing bikes has not increased. Do you think the manufacturer should be allowed to raise prices?"

It is worth highlighting the non-majority view here. Almost four in ten (39%) high school students said that companies should be allowed to raise their prices as demand increased. This minority group either understood abstractly that businesses thrive if they provide products that are in high demand, or perhaps they imagined themselves running a business and realized that, if they produced popular bicycles, they would want to sell each bicycle for what the market was willing to pay. Whatever explains these high school students' answers, they responded more like business owners.

Breaking down the high school students' responses by gender, race, and ethnicity reveals several perplexing differences (Table 5.3). First, young females are more likely than males to oppose the use of market forces to set prices (67% to 56%). A further indication of this difference is provided by the responses of males and females to the first question about government prohibiting price controls, although the data are not reported in table form. The results from the first question showed a similar, but a less pronounced difference (41% of females favored government intervention compared with 35% of males). The findings from both survey items on prices suggest that female youth may be thinking more like consumers rather than producers and may face more challenges to developing an entrepreneurial mindset than males, at least in regard to the function of markets and price determination.[4]

Table 5.3 Manufacturer Should Be Allowed to Raise Prices: High School[a]

| | **High School Students** | | | | | |
Response	**Total** (n=1010)	**Male** (444)	**Female** (566)	**White** (639)	**African American** (232)	**Hispanic** (205)
	%	%	%	%	%	%
Yes, allowed to	39	44	33	40	35	30
No, not allowed to	61	56	67	60	64	71
Don't know/Refused	0	0	0	–	0	–

Note: [a]"Suppose a bicycle manufacturer raises the price of bikes because the demand for them has increased even though the cost of producing bikes has not increased. Do you think the manufacturer should be allowed to raise prices?"

The results in Table 5.3 also indicate that Hispanic youth were less inclined to answer from an ownership mindset than any other group. A larger percentage of Hispanic youth (71%) would have disallowed manufacturers from reaping the rewards of creating a best-selling item compared with African Americans (64%) or whites (60%). Hispanic youth also showed similar differences on the first question on price controls (46% favored government intervention compared with 40% for African Americans and 36% for whites). Hispanic youth apparently are more influenced by thinking as consumers about prices, or they have less understanding about how markets determine prices (see Table 4.6). Their responses indicate that it will be more difficult for them to reconcile their perspectives on this matter with those of an entrepreneur when considering changes that affect prices in markets. Clearly, young Hispanics are at a distinct disadvantage when it comes to attitudes conducive to future entrepreneurial success.

Like high school students, the general public was divided on this question of price increases that are justified by increases in demand for a product. Slightly more than half (52%) of the general public answered the question from the perspective of consumers who did not want to pay more for a bicycle simply because it was popular. By contrast, slightly less than half (47%) of the general public recognized that businesses should be allowed to profit from popularity. Although these responses are generally similar to those of high school students in the fact that more supported price controls than were opposed to price controls, the percentages of the general public who supported and opposed were almost even. The general public, more so than high school students, had a greater appreciation of how a change in demand can be a legitimate reason for a price increase, probably because more members of the general public had work or business experience.

Predictably, business owners, who were the yardstick for measuring the entrepreneurial mentality when it came to this part of the interview, answered affirmatively more often than either high school students or the general public. The difference, as expected, was stark. Nearly seven in ten (69%) business owners answered "yes," of course, manufacturers should be allowed to raise prices if the demand supported higher prices! They probably understood the severe problems that occur in markets with price controls.

What was more surprising was that almost three in ten (29%) business owners replied that the bicycle producer should not profit from the popularity of his or her product. This result indicates that even business owners are not always well versed in economics or management, but it also raises the issue of why these particular business owners are in business for themselves in the first place if they do not seek to derive profit from increased demand for their goods or services. Perhaps some of them believed the increase in demand was temporary and thus did not substantiate the need for a price increase. It is also probably the case that they were thinking as consumers rather than as producers about the price implications from this demand shift.

A closer look at the data on business owners reveals that those with fewer employees were more likely to discount the relationship between profit and increased demand (Table 5.4). Those owners with 1–9 employees gave a "no" response 30% of the time, saying that manufacturers should not be allowed to raise prices. At the other end of the spectrum, business owners who employed between 10 and 49 employees answered "no" only 20–21% of the time. Also, about eight in ten (78–79%) business owners with 10–49 employees supported economic freedom for owners compared with only seven in ten (68%) owners with 1–9 employees. The number of employees appears to influence the ownership mindset.

Table 5.4 Manufacturer Should Be Allowed to Raise Prices: Business[a]

	Business Owners					
				Number of Employees		
Response	**Total** (n=403)	**Male** (296)	**Female** (107)	**1–9** (134)	**10–19** (134)	**20–49** (135)
	%	%	%	%	%	%
Yes, allowed to	69	76	51	68	79	78
No, not allowed to	29	22	47	30	21	20
Don't know/Refused	2	2	3	2	–	2

Note: [a]"Suppose a bicycle manufacturer raises the price of bikes because the demand for them has increased even though the cost of producing bikes has not increased. Do you think the manufacturer should be allowed to raise prices?"

The reason for this difference by number of employees is difficult to explain. Perhaps the smaller entrepreneurs in the study were in business sectors that did not give them firsthand experience with the scenario presented in this question. If an entrepreneur is not a manufacturer, for instance, he or she might distance himself or herself from this question. Many small business owners, for example, provide a service to a small number of reliable clients. They do not experience much increased demand or price fluctuation and therefore have no direct experience with the need to increase prices to both regulate and meet demand. It is also possible that these smaller business owners were more likely to lack education in management-related or economics topics, including how to most profitably set prices in response to increased demands from their clientele. Perhaps these businesses, partially as a result of the attitudes revealed in our study, were not charging enough for their goods or services for them to stay in business for the long run.

The other noteworthy difference is between male and female business owners. Female owners are more likely to oppose allowing prices to rise because of the increased demand than are male business owners (47% versus 22% opposed) and are significantly less likely to support giving businesses the freedom to raise prices in this situation (51% versus 76%). The results show that the thinking of female business owners is split about even on this issue whereas the great majority of male business owners favored giving the pricing freedom to the manufacturer. Some reasons given for why the results differ by the number of employees also probably apply to female owners of businesses. It may be the case that females are in businesses that are more oriented to customer loyalty and do not want to alienate them by appearing to take advantage of them by charging a higher price when demand increases.[5]

Overall, the results from the second interview question on how and when government was justified intervening in prices closely matched what might be expected. Despite the fact that high school students generally opposed price controls in the first hypothetical situation, they certainly supported them in the second. At least when it came to price controls, young people are still not thinking like entrepreneurs. A further test of the ownership mindset of teenagers involved questioning them about government regulation.

GOVERNMENT REGULATION

Government regulation of business is in some ways a more complicated issue than price controls because governments regulate businesses in a variety of ways that vary not only from state to state, but also from sector to sector. Regulations can enforce safety, protect the environment or control the raw materials used in products. Regulations also govern accounting procedures and reporting requirements for publicly held companies. In addition, regulatory regimes can structure markets themselves, such as when they include rules cable companies or energy monopolies must follow. Regulations can be both burdens and opportunities; they can stifle or promote competition, depending on how they are structured and enforced.

Time constraints and practical concerns, however, made it impossible to delve into regulatory issues with the interview respondents. Instead, this study could only broadly assess whether high school students' general views of government regulation were consonant with the views of most entrepreneurs by asking if they thought there was too much, too little, or about the right amount of government regulation. Of course the response to this one question does not address more complex issues such as what kind of regulation assists business, what kind of regulation restricts business, and what is the appropriate amount of regulation and time for it. When the respondents heard the term "regulation" they probably interpreted it in a pejorative way often portrayed in mass-market political discourse: rules and requirements businesses must follow – at a cost – to comply with a law.

Business owners comprise our baseline measure in this case, so it is instructive to review their responses. There was no right or wrong answer to this question. Its purpose was to draw a comparison among groups. Not surprisingly, given how most respondents probably interpreted our question, almost six in ten (56%) business owners said that there was too much government regulation (Table 5.5). Less than one in ten (7%) said that there was too little government regulation. About three in ten (32%) replied that government regulation was about right.

Table 5.5 Government Regulation of Business[a]

Response	High School Students (n=1,010)	General Public (n=607)	Business Owners (n=403)
Too much government regulation	22%	50%	56%
Too little government regulation	10	12	7
About the right amount of government regulation	66	34	32
Don't know/Refused	2	5	5

Note: [a]"Thinking about government regulation of business, do you think there is:"

Two-thirds (66%) of high school students had no complaint about government regulation of business and thought the amount of regulation was about right. This percentage was twice as high as the percentage of business owners (32%) who said they thought the amount of government regulation was about right. Less than a quarter (22%) of high school students, as opposed to more than half (56%) of business owners, thought government imposed too many regulations on business. The only similarity in the two groups was whether there was too little regulation. Ten percent of teenagers and 7% of business owners thought there was too little regulation.[6]

The difference between these two groups is sizable. One likely reason for this difference is that high school students do not experience the burden of government regulation. Their perspective on regulation is probably shaped as consumers who are supposed to be protected by government regulation and benefit from it. Unless there is a pressing consumer complaint about a product or business practice, it would be expected that most teenagers would think that the amount of government regulation was about right. In this case, youth are not thinking as business owners who may not want the regulatory intrusion that controls business practices and restricts freedom of operation. Most business owners understand the costs and consequences of government regulation for their businesses, and in general consider it to be excessive.

The general public held opinions similar to those of business owners about government regulation. Half (50%) of the general public, which was a slightly lower percentage than that of business owners (56%), thought there was too much government regulation. About one-third (34%) of the general public and about one-third (32%) of business owners stated that they thought there was just about the right amount of government regulation. Only about one in ten of each group thought there was too little government regulation.

The survey results provide several insights. First, regulation appears to be an issue for business owners and members of the general public in ways that it is not for high school students. This lack of concern about regulation is easily explained. Those individuals who don't own businesses do not experience the burden of government regulation that can be potentially onerous. High school students are simply ignorant of this dimension of business life. Compared to high school students, the general public is less ignorant, probably because they have more experience in working in businesses that have to deal with a regulatory burden. They may also be more informed on this issue from economic and financial news.

It is not surprising that most business owners think there is excessive government regulation. Complying with such regulations can be costly and less regulation can improve the return on investment for businesses. It is important to reiterate, however, that the purpose of this explanation is not to argue that government regulation of business is inappropriate or should be reduced in any particular case. The question simply asked for a general opinion about government regulation of business. A certain amount of government regulation of business is necessary, and it can enhance economic efficiency, especially in those markets where firms with monopoly powers would tend to distort competition. Government regulation also typically involves trade-offs between the economic goals of interest groups in a complex society. Businesses may need to be regulated by government if there are negative externalities resulting from production of a product and private markets do not adequately correct for such external costs.

What is salient here is that high school students do not share the concerns of business owners about over-regulation, although many of them aspire to be business owners themselves one day. This finding supplies further evidence that teenagers – even potential entrepreneurs – may lack an entrepreneurial mentality when it comes to the government's role of regulating businesses. On the other hand, it may be that high school students are unfamiliar with government regulation as it pertains to business and therefore by default they opt for the status quo. This lack of an entrepreneurial outlook or knowledge in this area constitutes another barrier young people must hurdle in the process of achieving their aspirations to own businesses.

TAXATION

The last question for assessing entrepreneurial mentality of teenagers asked about taxes. Like regulation, taxes are not a black-and-white issue. Taxation can take many forms. Taxes can be levied at the federal, state, or local level. There are income taxes and corporate taxes, payroll taxes, and capital gains taxes. Consumers pay taxes, as do producers. "Sin" taxes deliberately discourage consumption of particular products and raise substantial revenue, while other taxes only inadvertently stifle demand. Luxury taxes are predicated on the notion that the very wealthy can bear a greater tax burden, whereas specific tax breaks are often designed to encourage those with financial resources to invest in capital improvements and job creation.

Due to time constraints of the interview, only a general measure of sentiment about taxes could be used. One simple question was asked: "Thinking about taxes, do you think that most businesses are overtaxed, undertaxed, or taxed the right amount?" Similar to the previous question about regulation, the purpose in asking teenagers, the general public, and business owners their general opinion of taxation levels was to compare the attitudes toward taxation among the groups. The opinions of business owners regarding taxation were taken to be a benchmark against which we could compare the view of high school students.

As expected, given the fact that taxes are costs that cut into the income or revenue of businesses, the business owners who were surveyed in the study reported overwhelmingly that businesses were overtaxed. Over seven in ten (71%) business owners supplied this answer (Table 5.6). Only about two in ten (22%) business owners answered that businesses were taxed about the right amount. A negligible fraction (4%) of business owners stated that businesses were undertaxed. The opinion of business owners about taxation is unequivocal and clear: taxes are too high.

Table 5.6 Taxation[a]

Response	High School Students (n=1,010)	General Public (n=607)	Business Owners (n=403)
Overtaxed	46%	46%	71%
Undertaxed	9	15	4
Taxed about the right amount	41	32	22
Don't know/Refused	4	7	3

Note: [a]"Thinking about taxes, do you think that most businesses are:"

This pattern held within groups of business owners, subdivided by number of employees. The responses were similar across firms and ranged from 70%–75% depending on the number of employees. Interestingly, female business owners were the most uniform in their opinions that they were overtaxed. Eighty percent of female business owners said they were overtaxed compared with only 68% of male business owners who gave such a response. Only 15% of female business owners said they were taxed about the right amount compared with almost a quarter (24%) of male business owners.

High school students had ambivalent views of government regulation in large part because it did not directly affect or concern them. Taxes are a different matter. It was suspected that more people of all ages and walks of life had relatively developed opinions about taxes because almost everyone pays taxes in one form or another. Taxes are a part of everyday life. In addition, the anti-tax sentiment has a long history in the United States and teenage attitudes on this subject probably reflected the general attitude to some extent. On the other hand, the results from previous questions indicated how important it was to teenagers that businesses give back to their communities. Taxes, of course, are a universal way for businesses to do so. Therefore, it was conceivable, at least, that young people would hold opinions that businesses were not taxed enough.

As it turned out, high school students were fairly evenly split on the tax question. Over four in ten (46%) youth answered that they thought that businesses were overtaxed and another group of over four in ten (41%) youth responded that businesses were taxed about the right amount. Less than one in ten (9%) high school students answered that businesses were undertaxed. Not even high school students, who can be idealistic and naive in their thinking about business, were asking for increased taxes on businesses.[7]

The general public, on the other hand, had a more predictable distribution of opinion given the prevalence of anti-tax sentiment that is often expressed in local, state, or national debates on government spending by business and political leaders. Almost half (46%) of the general public said that businesses were overtaxed, the same percentage as youth. About one-third (32%) of the general public thought that businesses were taxed about the right amount, which is slightly less than the response given by youth. Like high school students, only a small percentage (15%) of the general public stated that businesses were undertaxed.

It is not surprising, given the broad and pervasive anti-tax mood found in public opinion in the United States, that the response that predominates from the choice set for all three groups was the opinion that businesses are overtaxed. Of course, it is the opinion of business owners that matters the most here, because in terms of the entrepreneurial mentality, the attitudes of business owners provide the benchmark, and also this is the group with the most direct experience with the issue. The findings show that high school students and business owners are far apart in their opinions about taxation, although the likely sentiment is similar in both groups.

In assessing the importance of this finding for future young entrepreneurs, it is hard to avoid the question of whether business owners are correct in their opinions about taxes. Are the owners of small businesses overtaxed, or, are they simply complaining about the reallocation of their income or revenue to government? Not only is answering this question beyond the scope of this study, but even if it was possible to provide a convincing answer, it would not help in assessing the obstacles young entrepreneurs face in developing an ownership mindset. This realization occurs because the purpose of the study is not to advocate a dramatic change in tax policy in the United States. Nor is it particularly likely that individual business owners can be convinced that they should feel good about paying more taxes. Assuming conditions remain as they are – taxes do not dramatically decrease and taxpayers remain unenthusiastic about paying taxes – what should be the concern with the attitudes of teenagers' attitudes toward business taxes?

If business tax levels turn out to be a disincentive for young people to go into business for themselves, then they should be a target of concern. There is no evidence, however, of such an adverse effect on entrepreneurial inclinations on the part of high school students. Taxation does not seem to discourage young people from being interested in business. Their interest is based on the promise of economic autonomy and self-actualization. Taxes do not appear to be a substantial counterweight to those advantages.

More realistically, teenagers' attitudes toward business taxation are probably a product of their lack of experience and knowledge. As some of these high school students strive to accomplish their dreams to initiate ventures, they likely will develop a more critical attitude toward the business taxes they will pay.

CONCLUSION

In exploring the fit between the mentality of the aspiring teenage entrepreneur and the existing business owner, the findings show that high school students' attitudes toward government, markets, regulations, and taxes do not closely match those of business owners. High school students are *much less likely* than business owners to think that businesses are overburdened with government regulation and that business taxes are too high. The less negative attitude of high school students toward government regulation of business may be related to their lack of business or work experience or their lack of knowledge about government regulation. The typical high school response about taxes is probably due to the same factors, or perhaps it indicates a more accepting attitude toward the government taking a share of business revenue to help pay for public goods and services. The most striking difference in the thinking of high school students and business owners is the relatively high percentage of teenagers who support price controls that limit the power of businesses to price their goods or services, especially due to an increase in demand for a product. The attitude on price controls may simply represent a lack of economic knowledge, but it more likely arises from consumer-oriented aversion to a price increase for any product and indicates that teenagers have difficulty thinking as producers. Overall, the attitude and opinion evidence shows that the ownership mindset is missing from many aspiring entrepreneurs. Youth may be ill-prepared to deal with or surprised by these issues when they want to start businesses.

Even if these attitudes toward government, markets, regulation, and taxes cannot be attributed simply to ignorance or naiveté, they can be addressed with education. Assuming over half of the students interviewed are serious about their intentions to some day work for themselves, nothing that was presented in this chapter should be an *insurmountable* obstacle to the chances for many youth to achieve their goals of starting their own businesses. The next chapter addresses these concerns by discussing the topic of entrepreneurship education and what it can contribute to youth to prepare them for an entrepreneurial world.

NOTES

1. There are many books that describe, discuss, and analyze entrepreneurial characteristics, traits, or mentalities. For several examples, see Ericksen (1997), and McGrath and MacMillan (2000).
2. See Walstad and Kourilsky (1999), pp. 74–80.
3. There are also some subtle differences by gender and ethnicity. Many young females express more support to having the government restrict prices than do young males (41% versus 35%). Hispanics also express more support for government intervention (46%) when compared with whites (36%) or African American youth (40%). The differences between males and females or for Hispanic youth become greater when the second survey item on prices is asked (see Table 5.3).

4. For a discussion of factors affecting the opinions of young females about government and markets, see Walstad and Kourilsky (1999), p. 80, and Kourilsky and Walstad (2005), pp. 29–34. In particular, Kourilsky and Walstad (2005) discuss in detail the challenges and solutions to developing more entrepreneurship among female youth.
5. Female views of entrepreneurship are also discussed in Kourilsky and Walstad (2005).
6. The differences in the responses to this item by gender, race, or ethnicity are essentially the same as for the overall total for youth.
7. There are some differences by gender, race, and ethnicity on this item, but the magnitudes are not large. Female youth are more likely than male youth to state that businesses are overtaxed (50% versus 43%). Also, African American youth are more likely than whites to state that businesses are overtaxed (54% versus 44%), and so are Hispanic youth (48%).

6. Entrepreneurship Education

Throughout this book the analysis has shown that high school students who aspire to economic autonomy face attitudinal and knowledge barriers to achieving this goal. This chapter argues that the educational system in this country, to the extent that it does little to remove knowledge barriers, can be considered a passive impediment to youth entrepreneurship. Data presented here establish that educational opportunities for entrepreneurship are sparser than high school students, members of the general public, or business owners state they would like them to be. High school students, however, know the importance of entrepreneurship education to their economic achievement, and thus seek access to these learning opportunities.

As explained in this chapter, high school students say they receive little preparation in high school for someday initiating their own business ventures. Many of these teenagers also report that they are interested in learning more, would be interested in a variety of different kinds of instructional opportunities, are willing to devote substantial time to this pursuit of knowledge, and believe strongly that the schools should do more. This information can be used to draw the outlines of an educational reform that will satisfy the demand for a curriculum that does more to prepare U.S. youth for an entrepreneurial life and thereby encourages and increases entrepreneurship in the economy and economic mobility for youth.

HIGH SCHOOL COURSEWORK

The results from Chapter 4 showed that high school students lacked knowledge of concepts related to entrepreneurship, business, and economics. The average percentage correct on the knowledge test was only 52% for high school students (see Table 4.1). Such a score is a strong indicator that many youth lack basic knowledge or understanding of entrepreneurship and related concepts that would help them start and grow businesses.

In addition, high school students were well aware that their knowledge of starting and managing a business was limited. In fact, three in ten (30%) students gave themselves a poor or very poor rating on such knowledge and almost five in ten (47%) only considered it to be fair. Only about two in ten (22%) students rated their knowledge of starting and managing a business as either good or excellent (see Table 4.8). These self-ratings provide further corroboration that many youth are not educated for entrepreneurship.

The follow-up questions explored some reasons for this situation. Perhaps it occurred because many teenagers failed to receive any direct instruction in entrepreneurship, business, economics, or related subjects in school. Perhaps many high school students had taken courses in such subjects, but the courses did not provide them with the important skills and knowledge they would need for success in establishing their own ventures. It may also have been the case that these skills and knowledge were not retained.

One way to find out what courses were taken by youth in high school was to ask them. Questions were included on the survey to ask the interviewees who had attended high school to indicate whether they had taken a course in business or entrepreneurship, a course in economics, or a course in personal finance or consumer economics in high school. The respondents were also asked whether they had participated in an extracurricular or community program on entrepreneurship while they were attending high school.

The data on coursework should be interpreted with caution. On the one hand, students may *overstate* the amount of coursework taken because they do not have an accurate memory. For example, an economics course might be thought of as a course in personal finance or consumer economics, or vice versa. Some students may also answer "yes" to taking more courses than were completed because they remember instruction about the topic even if it was not in a separate and well-defined course. On the other hand, the sampling may *understate* the eventual amount of coursework taken by high school students because the average age of the students surveyed was 16 and some students had not yet completed taking all their coursework. This factor, however, would be offset by any students who dropped out of high school in their junior or senior year in high school. The major point is that the data on coursework should be considered an estimate of the relative magnitude of the exposure of high school students to such courses.

As shown in Table 6.1, about three in ten (30%) of high school youth reported taking a course in either business or entrepreneurship. These data suggest that the vast majority (70%) of high school students do not participate in the type of direct coursework that would give them even the basic knowledge or skills to prepare for the world of business, and much less for starting a business.

Table 6.1 Education in High School[a]

Response	High School Students (n=1,010)	General Public (n=587)[b]	Business Owners (n=403)[b]
A. A course in economics	39%	46%	34%
B. A course in business or entrepreneurship	30	27	17
C. A course in personal finance or consumer economics	27	29	22
D. An extracurricular or community program on entrepreneurship	14	10	10

Notes:
[a]"In high school, have you taken or are you currently taking:"
[b]For respondents who attended high school.

One difficulty with the survey is that the question on coursework in high school did not make a distinction between taking business courses of a general or skill nature or taking a course in entrepreneurship. Both types of courses were lumped together as one response. Most likely, when youth reported taking a course in business or entrepreneurship, it was a course in introduction to business, general management, or a computer skills course that was taught in a business department of a high school. There may be few students who took a high school course in entrepreneurship, and even if such a course was taken, little is known about the focus, content, or quality of that course.[1]

Less than half the percentage who said they completed a course in business or entrepreneurship in high school stated that they had participated in an extracurricular or community program in entrepreneurship (14%). Such programs can be useful for helping students to get started on the path to entrepreneurship in those circumstances where direct instruction in school is not offered. The findings for the extracurricular programs unfortunately reveal that this indirect instruction outside of school classrooms is not a significant source of entrepreneurship education for high school students.[2]

Potential entrepreneurs also can benefit from the knowledge and skills taught in courses in personal finance. These courses cover topics such as earning income, spending decisions, budgeting, taxes, insurance, saving, and investing. These courses also focus on personal decision-making, and this focus can be of value to potential entrepreneurs because decisions about personal finance can be similar to the types of business decisions that potential entrepreneurs must make. The survey results show that instruction in personal finance is limited. Just over one-fourth (27%) of high school students reported taking a personal finance course in high school. As a consequence, most students cannot use a personal finance route to develop the skills or knowledge that also would have some application to the development of business and entrepreneurial knowledge and skills.

An economics course can also be of value to future entrepreneurs. In an ideal world, an economics course for high school students covers basic principles of macroeconomics and microeconomics. The macro portion of the course explains how the national or international economy works. The micro portion explains how private markets determine prices and allocate resources. An economics course also explains the economic effects of different market structures in which businesses operate. In theory, such an economics course can provide future entrepreneurs with a broader and deeper understanding of how market forces influence prices, production, and innovation, and how economic factors affect the national and international economies.[3] The results showed that an economics course is taken by a plurality (39%) of high school students, the most among the options listed.[4]

The findings for the general public corroborate the findings from high school students for the most part. About the same percentages of the general public took a course in business and entrepreneurship (27%), a course in personal finance (29%), or participated in an extracurricular or community program in entrepreneurship while in high school as did the sample of high school students. It is clear that neither high school students nor the general public received much coursework in subjects that could contribute to the development of their entrepreneurial knowledge or skills.

More of the general public reported taking a course in economics (46%) than did high school students (39%). The difference is probably attributable to the fact that economics, more so than the other courses discussed above, is often taught during the senior year in high school, so the high school percentages would be expected to rise if more of the high school sample had completed their senior year. This estimate is about the same as an estimate obtained from transcript data on economics courses for high school graduates.[5] It suggests that about half of the nation's teenagers do not take an economics course in high school – a course that could have enlightened them on how markets can and do operate, and how the national and international economies work.

Not only was it important to know what entrepreneurship-related courses were taken commonly in high school, but also whether business owners had received any formal instruction in economic, financial, or entrepreneurship concepts in high school. What differentiated business owners from the other two groups in terms of their education? Was it possible that entrepreneurs had been either fortunate enough or sufficiently self-possessed to pursue learning opportunities in high school even as other high school students missed these opportunities?

Interestingly, smaller percentages of small business owners reported having taken courses in business or entrepreneurship (17%), personal finance (22%), or economics (34%) compared to the other two groups. The reason for the difference is most likely due to the age of the samples. The average age of the business owner was 51 and the median was 49. The general public sample was younger, with an average age of 44 and a median age of 43. What this difference means is that business owners, for the most part, were educated in a period of time when there were fewer high school students who took such courses.[6]

The coursework data for small business owners reveals that many individuals who initiate businesses may be starting their ventures with "one hand tied behind their back." They also were aware of this lack of knowledge of starting and managing a business at the time they started their businesses, based on self-rating data (Table 4.8). Over one-third (37%) of business owners rated their knowledge as poor or very poor at the time they started their businesses. One-third (34%) rated their knowledge of starting and managing a business as only fair. Less than one-third (29%) gave themselves a good or excellent rating.

This lack of knowledge and know-how may be just one of the explanations for why so many businesses fail, and perhaps could have been remedied or at least substantially mitigated by education that begins in high school. This entrepreneurship education may be especially important for prospective entrepreneurs because the data from the business owners show that half (50%) had less than a four-year college degree: almost a quarter (23%) had only a high school education or less, and over a quarter (27%) had some postsecondary education, but did not earn a four-year degree.

Worth re-emphasizing is that only a minority of any of the three groups ever took a business, personal finance, or economics course or participated in an entrepreneurship-related program in high school. This evidence indicates that there is a substantial deficit in entrepreneurship-related courses in the U.S. secondary schools' curricula and – even when they do exist – prospective entrepreneurs are not being counseled to take these courses.

A further breakdown of the high school sample (Table 6.2) shows that African American students were more likely than their white peers to have taken entrepreneurship-related courses. These results again document that African American youth seem oriented toward entrepreneurship more often than other groups and seek learning opportunities when available. These results suggest that African American high school students are more likely to take courses in high school relating to their entrepreneurship aspirations.

Table 6.2 Education in High School by Characteristics[a]

| Response | High School Students | | | | | |
	Total (n=1010)	Male (444)	Female (566)	White (639)	African American (232)	Hispanic (205)
	%	%	%	%	%	%
A. A course in economics	39	40	37	38	46	37
B. A course in business or entrepreneurship	30	32	27	27	41	31
C. A course in personal finance or consumer economics	27	29	25	24	37	31
D. An extracurricular or community program on entrepreneurship	14	16	13	13	20	17

Note: [a]"In high school, have you taken or are you currently taking:"

One good reason for this greater level of coursework among African American youth in entrepreneurship-related subjects is that they show much greater interest in starting businesses than their white counterparts. Over three-fourths (77%) of African American youth preferred starting their own business over working for someone else (Table 2.1). Three-fourths (75%) of African American youth said they would like to start their own businesses (Table 2.1). Two-thirds (67%) of African American youth stated they were likely to act on their entrepreneurial aspirations (Table 2.3).

HIGHER EDUCATION

Courses and programs in colleges and universities also can be a source of education to prepare people for entrepreneurship. The survey included a question about coursework in entrepreneurship and related subjects in college (Table 6.3). The general public sample contained about half (51%) who had some type of college education: attended college, but received no degree (18%); a two-year college degree (9%); a four-year college degree (14%); and, postgraduate work (10%). As might be expected, the business owner sample showed a higher level of education than the general public. Three-fourths (75%) of business owners had some type of college education: attended college, but received no degree (15%); only a two-year college degree (10%); only a four-year college degree (33%); and, postgraduate work (17%).

Table 6.3 Education in College[a]

Response	General Public (n=311)[b]	Business Owners (n=301)[b]
A. A course in small business or entrepreneurship	17%	27%
B. Other business courses[c]	58	61
C. A course in economics	50	62
D. An extracurricular or community program on entrepreneurship	15	15

Notes:
[a]"In high school, have you taken or are you currently taking:"
[b]For respondents who attended high school.
[c]Such as accounting, business law, finance, management, and marketing.

It is at the college or university level where many owners of small businesses clearly received instruction in entrepreneurship-related subjects. Courses in either business or economics were the most common ones taken. Over six in ten (61–62%) business owners took either an economics course in college or took other business courses such as accounting, business law, finance, management, and marketing. A minority (27%) of business owners also prepared for their careers as entrepreneurs by taking a specific course on small business management or entrepreneurship. A few (15%) business owners participated in an extracurricular or community program on entrepreneurship.

These results were not unexpected. Colleges and universities typically offer career-related instruction in business and related subjects. College students, who naturally are more career-oriented than younger high school students, select from among different paths of study based partially on their planned careers. Those college students who plan to own businesses someday would be expected to take business courses in preparation for going into business for themselves. Most high school students, however, often do not have access to such coursework and they may not have the opportunity to receive entrepreneurship-related instruction especially if they never attend a college or university.

Predictably, the sub-sample of the general public who had some type of college education took fewer courses in small business and entrepreneurship, other business subjects, or economics, but the differences were not all that large. Less than two in ten (17%) had taken a specific course to prepare them in business, such as small business management or entrepreneurship. Few (15%) had participated in an extracurricular or community program on entrepreneurship. The general public was much more likely to have taken other business courses (58%) or an economics course (50%). It appeaɪ those members of the general public as well as business owners who able to attend college had more access to those learning opportunities ᴜɪaᴛ would have in all likelihood proved helpful in starting a business than those high school students who never attend a college or university.

YEARNING FOR LEARNING

As discussed above, data from the interviews demonstrated both a general lack of entrepreneurship-related knowledge among teenagers (see Chapter 4) and evidence that a majority of teenagers do not take courses related to entrepreneurship in high school. Perhaps one explanation for those results is that little demand exists for such educational opportunities, but it can be dismissed because of the great interest in entrepreneurship expressed by high school students. To account for why so few teenagers took entrepreneurship-related classes it was necessary to know whether students were interested in learning more about entrepreneurship in school, so such a question was asked (Table 6.4). In response, two-thirds (67%) of high school students said yes that they wanted to learn more about entrepreneurship and starting a business.

Table 6.4 Interest in Learning More about Entrepreneurship[a]

Response	High School Students (n=1,010)	General Public (n=607)
Yes	67%	40%
No	32	60
Don't know/Refused	1	0

Note: [a]"Would you be interested in learning more about entrepreneurship or starting a business?"

The question was asked of the general public to measure whether there was interest in learning opportunities that were not connected necessarily to their enrolling in programs at educational institutions. The general public was considerably less interested than high school students. Four in ten (40%) said yes and six in ten (60%) said no. This response may be because many adults consider their education complete after secondary school or postsecondary school. Alternatively, some in the general public may already have chosen another career path and did not see the value of such education.

The conclusion to be drawn from reviewing the results from both samples is that interest in learning more about entrepreneurship will be at its highest peak among youth. It will diminish as youth become adults because there are other interests, other career paths, the pressure of family, or some other influence that changes the thinking of people so that fewer of them consider entrepreneurship to be a viable possibility and worth learning more about.

This interest in learning more about entrepreneurship is also consistent with interest in becoming an entrepreneur. In this regard, the general public was split in their interest in starting or not starting a business compared with an overwhelming response from youth, with almost two-thirds who wanted to start businesses and only one-third were not interested (Table 2.2). The reason a greater number of high school students want to learn more about entrepreneurship is because a larger percentage of that group wants to start businesses than is the case with the general public.

On this item, the sample of African American students differs from white students. African American youth show exceptional interest (82%) in learning more about entrepreneurship and starting a business compared with white youth (63%). These results correspond to other findings related to African American youth and entrepreneurship that were reported throughout this study. Not only do African American students express more interest in entrepreneurship (Table 2.2) and a higher likelihood of acting on their aspirations (Table 2.3), but also they seek educational opportunities that will provide them with entrepreneurial skills and knowledge.

Overall, the findings that two-thirds of high school students claim an interest in learning more about entrepreneurship, combined with the coursework findings that show only limited taking of courses related to an entrepreneurship education, suggests that something prevents interested students from pursuing this particular educational goal. The data in this study do not reveal what the barriers may be, but some possibilities are that the courses simply are not available, they are offered in such a way that access to them is limited, or when they are taught they are presented in a boring manner, and word-of-mouth may dissuade others from taking such courses.

MODES OF DELIVERY

Given the greater interest among high school students than the general public in acquiring entrepreneurial knowledge, it would be reasonable to suggest that high school classes would be the appropriate place to provide this type of instruction. Did evidence substantiate this speculation? Educational life for many high school students is filled with courses and activities necessary for completion of graduation requirements and life after high school. It was conceivable to think that high school students were cognizant of their own limitations and might be uninterested in more schoolwork. Even if they were resistant to more courses in school, it was important to know if high school students also were resistant to alternative formats of entrepreneurship education, or whether learning entrepreneurship-related skills via the Internet or using other communications media in addition to, or outside of, the high school was something which students would consider doing. Of course, another possibility was that these interested students may have been planning to defer their entrepreneurial education until college.

For the purposes of making a successful recommendation that was both feasible and appealing to youth, the next question sought to reveal preferences for participation in entrepreneurship education. The question was asked only of those high school students and members of the general public who had indicated an interest in learning more in their response to the preceding question. In responding to the query regarding what format they preferred, interviewees had several options from which to select: taking a course in college; taking a course in high school; attending an extracurricular or community program; watching a video, DVD, or CD-ROM; or participating in an online program through the Internet.

Nearly all high school students stated that they would be willing to take a high school course (92%) or a college course (95%). In fact, majorities of high school students said they were interested in all means of learning more about starting a business. Over seven in ten (74%) said they were willing to participate in a community or extracurricular program, over six in ten (61%) were willing to watch a video, and over five in ten (53%) were willing to participate in an online program (Table 6.5).

Table 6.5 Means for Learning More about Entrepreneurship[a]

Response	High School Students (n=670)[b]	General Public (n=235)[b]
Taking a course in college, if you plan to attend college	95%	82%
Taking a course in high school	92	–
Attending an extracurricular or community program	74	86
Watching a video, DVD, or CD-ROM	61	73
Participating in an online program through the Internet	53	65

Notes:
[a]"Through what means would you be willing to learn more about entrepreneurship and starting a business?"
[b]For YES respondents to being interested in learning more about entrepreneurship.

Among the general public who were interested in learning more about entrepreneurship, there was enthusiasm that was similar to that of high school students. In fact, the interested general public was more willing than even high school students to attend a program (86%), watch a video, DVD, or CD-ROM (73%) and participate in an online program. They were only somewhat less willing (82%) to take a college course.

Although not reported in table form, the results from African American youth reveal some subtle differences when compared with white youth. Both African American and white students expressed a great willingness (94% and 96%) to take a course in high school and also great willingness (92% and 94%) to take a college course, if planning to attend college. Where the two groups differed was on the other options. African American youth were more interested than white youth in extracurricular programs (83% versus 70%), watching a video, DVD, or CD-ROM program (70% versus 58%), and in participating in an online program using the Internet (66% versus 50%). The great majority of African American youth showed interest in learning about entrepreneurship regardless of the mode of delivery of the education.

The findings show that many high school students and the general public are open to learning more about starting a business through means that did not necessarily involve traditional instruction. The next question to be asked was how much time the respondents were willing to devote to each of the alternative modalities for learning. An indication of the time investment individuals were willing to make also could be read as a sign of the importance they attached to learning more about entrepreneurship. In addition, it was valuable to know if high school students in particular were interested in augmenting their studies by allocating additional instructional time to participate in extracurricular programs, watching electronic programs on starting businesses, or by taking Internet-based entrepreneurship courses. The general public and high school students were asked how long they were willing to spend on each instructional format. When responding to this question, interviewees selected one of several time allocations: one hour or less, two hours, three hours, or four or more hours.[7]

The non-course format for instruction to which the majority of high school students were willing to devote the most time was extracurricular programs on entrepreneurship (Table 6.6). When the hour allocation was split into two main categories (1–2 or 3+), almost half (48%) of youth were willing to devote three or more hours to this form of instruction. The modality warranting the next highest time allocation was an online program, for which one-third (34%) were willing to spend three or more hours. The format that drew the lowest time commitment was the DVD, or video-based program with only 17% thinking it was worth three or more hours.

Table 6.6 Hours Willing to Do Programs on Entrepreneurship[a]

	1	2	3	4+	DK
Attend an extracurricular or community program on entrepreneurship[b]					
High school students (n=522)	19%	28%	10%	38%	5%
General public (n=201)	5	16	8	63	8
Watch a video, DVD, or CD-Rom program on entrepreneurship[b]					
High school students (n=418)	51%	30%	7%	10%	3%
General public (n=165)	30	34	5	27	5
Participate in online program on entrepreneurship through the Internet[b]					
High school students (n=365)	36%	25%	11%	24%	4%
General public (n=150)	12	19	12	50	7

Notes:
[a]"For how many hours would you be willing to:"
[b]For YES respondent to the specific program.

The answers teenagers gave to these questions may reveal a certain level of sophistication in assessing the strengths and weaknesses of various instructional formats. It should not be taken as a rejection of the video format, for instance, that few students wanted to devote many hours to this type of instruction. Videos are fairly passive forms of instruction and designed for an efficient transmission of factual information that can be conveyed in a relatively short period. Over eight in ten (81%) high school students, probably because of extensive experience with instructional videos and with movie entertainment, said they would be willing to allocate one or two hours to this format. This time frame is arguably the most appropriate and the higher end of two hours corresponds with what youth typically experience when they go to see movies for entertainment purposes. The results of this interview question suggest that this is a case of the students knowing best how to allocate instructional time and effort.

The general public, no doubt reflecting their different life situations, expressed time allocation preferences for types of instruction that differed substantially from those of high school students. Among the four in ten (40%) of the general public who were interested in learning more about entrepreneurship, large percentages were willing to allocate time to a number of different types of instruction. About seven in ten (71%) were willing to devote either three hours (8%) or four or more hours (63%) to an extracurricular or community program. Instruction through watching a video, DVD or CD-ROM program attracted less of a prospective time commitment from the general public, with about two-thirds (64%) prepared to devote only one hour (30%) or two hours (34%) to this type of instruction. Instruction via the Internet, however, attracted a willingness to commit more time. About two-thirds (60%) were prepared to give either three hours (12%) or four or more hours (50%) to this instructional medium.

One might anticipate that the general public would be more attracted to Internet instruction than were high school students considering that many members of the general public probably have schedules that make classroom instruction difficult. Working adults are the major market for distance and non-traditional, non-residence educational programs. Of course, high school students – many of whom do not work outside their schools – have time for day classes. Thus, these time allocation findings lend support to an instructional strategy that calls for reaching out to students wherever they "live." If high school students are the target audience, then high school is the appropriate venue for entrepreneurship courses.

This information on the types of education high school students prefer, and how much time they are willing to devote to different instructional formats, provides the curriculum designer with an outline of a possible schedule of a successful entrepreneurship education program. The findings indicate that although they are most willing to take a class in high school or college if they plan to attend college, three-quarters of high school students also are willing to participate in an extracurricular program that meets on weekends or after school perhaps for an hour or two, one or two days a week. Such a program might include an online component and require students to watch a DVD or work through a CD-ROM as part of the course materials, but these formats should probably not occupy the majority of instructional time.[8] More consideration is given to planning and executing entrepreneurship education for high school students in the final chapter.

A STRONG RECOMMENDATION

From the data presented so far in this book – from interest, through lack of knowledge, lack of access, and propensity to learn more – the conclusion is that entrepreneurship education is important to teenagers. The interest of teenagers in entrepreneurship is founded on a strong desire to achieve economic autonomy. Of course, many barriers stand in the way of young people joining the ranks of successful entrepreneurs. No matter how these obstacles are explained and categorized, however, they essentially come down to a lack of educational opportunity. What accounts for this lack of opportunity given an interest in entrepreneurship, a demonstrated lack of knowledge, or "need to know more," and the demand from high school students? Is the will for a policy change missing? High school students clearly have desire, needs, and aspirations, but they do not have a great deal of influence over curricular decisions. Thus, it also was important to know if the general public, which is the actual constituency of public schools, supported the notion that public schools should provide entrepreneurship-related classes.

There could be a wide range of opinion on this item, so rather than simply asking for a yes or no response on whether it was important for the schools to teach about entrepreneurship, the respondents were asked to rate their views on the importance of schools to provide entrepreneurship education. The scale ranged from one to five, where a five denoted "very important" and one was "not at all important." To compare the ratings of high school students on the importance of entrepreneurship education to the responses reflecting the opinions of the general public and to those of business owners, the same question was asked the same way to both groups.

Based on the findings so far in the study, it was anticipated that high school students would place a high degree of importance on the nation's schools teaching entrepreneurship for the simple reason that, as students in high schools, these teenagers naturally would look to their current surroundings as the place to learn more about any subject of interest. Therefore, it was not surprising that over eight in ten (81%) of high school students responded that it was either very important (49%) or important (32%) for the nation's schools to teach students about entrepreneurship and starting a business (Table 6.7). Though this result was expected, it nevertheless stands out as dramatic and incontrovertible evidence that teenagers would support a curriculum change or enhancement in their high

Table 6.7 Importance of Teaching about Entrepreneurship in Schools[a]

Response	High School Students (n=1,010)	General Public (n=607)	Business Owners (n=403)
5 Very important	49%	59%	73%
4	32	22	15
3	14	14	7
2	3	2	2
1 Not at all important	2	3	2

Note: [a]"Using a five-point scale, where 5 is very important, and 1 is not at all important, how important is it for our nation's schools to teach students about entrepreneurship and starting a business?"

schools. Less than two in ten (19%) answered with a neutral response (14%) or thought this type of education was not important (3%), or not at all important (2%).

Although it was expected that high school students would say that it was important that schools provide entrepreneurship education, it was anticipated that the general public would be less enthusiastic. As adults who were likely familiar with a range of educational experiences, the general public may not have asked that the school system take on this task. Therefore, it was somewhat unexpected that the general public stated even more strongly than high school students that the nation's schools should teach about entrepreneurship and starting a business. Like high school students, eight in ten (81%) of the general public thought it was either very important (59%) or important (22%) for the schools to provide this entrepreneurship education. In fact, the percentage giving it the highest ranking of very important (59%) was greater than even the percentage of high school students (49%) giving it same highest ranking.

But if both high school students themselves and members of the general public saw value in schools providing entrepreneurship education, business owners were even more strongly disposed to valuing this proposition. Almost nine in ten business owners (88%) rated the importance of our nation's schools teaching students about entrepreneurship and starting a business as either very important (73%) or important (15%). In this case the response of business owners was even more enthusiastic and supportive for having the nation's schools teach about entrepreneurship and starting a business than that found with the general public or high school students as measured by the percentages stating it was very important.

Given an opportunity to express their views, the consistent response from each group was that the teaching of entrepreneurship was considered to be an important responsibility of the nation's schools. About five in ten (49%) high school students, six in ten (59%) of the general public, and over seven in ten (73%) of business owners saw offering this kind of education as "very important" for the nation's schools. The only differences among the three groups were in the percentages of each group that designated teaching entrepreneurship as very important compared with the percentages who stated it was important. It is interesting that although teenagers strongly demand the chance to learn entrepreneurship, the general public and business owners expressed even stronger support for having the nation's schools provide entrepreneurship education for students.

CONCLUSION

In the face of the preceding evidence, a pressing question is whether, despite the findings of this study, institutional, historical, or cultural barriers stand in the way of offering entrepreneurship education as a more substantial component of the nation's secondary school curricula. Is it simply inertia that maintains the status quo? One consideration is that adding entrepreneurship education to the high school curriculum is not without controversy. Currently, the secondary school curriculum focuses almost exclusively on teaching general subjects: knowledge that is intended to help everyone no matter what they plan to do in the future. School administrators and teachers have not yet realized that entrepreneurial thinking falls into this category. Instead, they associate entrepreneurship education with vocational education, which has fallen out of favor in the nation's schools.[9]

The preceding chapters have established (using accumulated evidence from studies of high school students, the general public, and business owners which have been conducted over an eight-year period) that there is a strong interest in entrepreneurship and a strong demand for entrepreneurship education. The need of young people to achieve economic autonomy in the current climate of global challenges is greater than ever as the prospect of prosperity derived from taking a well-paying job with stable employment rapidly vanishes. Moreover, for many less-advantaged youth, perhaps from immigrant families or historically underserved minority groups, the need to provide access to entrepreneurial opportunity is even greater.

The data presented in this book show that teenagers themselves have ownership aspirations and are aware of the educational barriers that stand in their way. These young people are mindful also of their own shortcomings in the areas of economics and business management knowledge and they have declared their interest and willingness to undertake educational programs that will provide them with the desired knowledge. Furthermore, they agree with small business owners and the general public that the nation's schools should provide these educational programs.

From all this, it should be clear that a curricular reform in the nation's high schools that accomplishes the goal of providing high school students with access to entrepreneurship education that will allow them to realize their goals of establishing their own for-profit or not-for-profit enterprises will in all likelihood attract a large and receptive audience. Given this need and demand for such an educational initiative, the question becomes how to proceed. The response is to listen to the voices of students. The data presented in this chapter help find those voices and contribute to the design of such a program.

There is a strong basis for placing entrepreneurship education in high schools for the simple reason that high school students are intent at some point in the future on becoming their own bosses, interested in the subject and willing to devote time to its study. Because the general public is relatively less interested than high school students in acquiring entrepreneurship-related skills and knowledge, reaching individuals during their teenage years is a strategic alternative for expanding the entrepreneurial economy.

NOTES

1. The percentages reported by students may be overstated based on high school transcripts. Walstad and Rebeck (2000) found that only about 15% of high school graduates took a course in general business and only 3% took a course in entrepreneurship. A review of legislation on the teaching of entrepreneurship concepts in the public school curriculum found only nine states with statutes (Zinth 2007).
2. Another issue is similar to the one stated about business or entrepreneurship courses in high school. Nothing is known about the focus, content, or quality of such extracurricular or community programs even if they are completed by students.
3. Economics courses may deviate substantially from this ideal description, and in practice, the teaching of economics can vary substantially across school districts and states (see Walstad 2001).
4. These survey estimates for economics may understate the amount of coursework in this subject. Walstad and Rebeck (2000) used data on actual transcripts for high school students and found the percentage taking a well-defined economics course to be about 44% in 1994. It may have risen closer to 50% by 2005 because of more state or school district mandates for such courses (see NCEE 2005).
5. See the previous endnote for this transcript estimate.
6. Most of these business owners were educated in high school during the mid-1960s to mid-1970s when there was much less coursework taken in economics or the other subjects. Walstad (1992) discusses the historical trends in such coursework.
7. No questions were asked to ascertain whether the number of hours indicated were in addition to or instead of classroom instruction.
8. The responses of high school students on questions of curriculum suggest that alternatives to providing this type of education in the schools should be explored. For example, community college classes offered to high school students may be an option worth investigating.

Alternative modalities also can be used or incorporated. Distance learning solutions are likely to find a receptive audience, but they probably should be implemented as components of programs that also include face-to-face elements. High school students are willing to spend some time online or viewing videos, but they appeared in our data to be more comfortable with the more traditional instructional formats.

9. Benavot (1983) provides an international perspective on the decline of vocational education in the 1970s. This decline continued and accelerated through the mid-1990s, as documented in the most recent NCES report on vocational education (Levesque, Lauen, et al. 2000).

7. A Longitudinal Perspective and the Major Findings

The previous five chapters presented an analysis of data from interviews with representative samples of young people, the general public, and business owners. The data, however, were collected at a point in time: the fall of 2002. A follow-up question to be asked about the findings is whether these cross-sectional results from one year are consistent with any past findings, or whether there have been significant variations or changes over time in the thinking or responses of youth, the general public, or small business owners.

Fortunately, this follow-up question can be answered for the most part because many of the questions used in the current survey also were asked in 1994 interviews that were conducted with national random samples of high school students, the general public, and business owners.[1] The availability of prior data on a large set of the same or similar questions that also were administered to the three groups in 2002 make it possible to conduct a longitudinal comparison on five major topics discussed in the five previous chapters: interest, philanthropy, knowledge, mindsets, and education.

The first purpose of this chapter, therefore, is to assess whether the views, opinions, and knowledge of entrepreneurship shown by high school students, the general public, or business owners changed substantially over the intervening eight years when the two surveys were conducted. This trend analysis will be essential for determining whether the 2002 results, so extensively described and presented in earlier chapters, have general validity over time, and are not unique to one year or an exception to past findings.

With this longitudinal perspective in mind, it will then be worthwhile to return to the 2002 results and provide a summary of findings as a second purpose of this chapter. The volume of survey data and reporting of results already presented may obscure the more important findings. This concise summary of the major findings will serve as a prelude to the discussions of the implications and extrapolations described in the next chapter.

INTEREST IN ENTREPRENEURSHIP

In 1994, high school students, the general public, and business owners were asked the hypothetical question: "If you had the choice between being a small business owner or a manager in a large corporation, which would you rather be?" Almost six in ten (59%) high school students, over seven in ten (73%) of the general public, and almost nine in ten (89%) small business owners said they preferred to be an owner of a small business when given this choice. These survey results clearly showed that there was a strong interest in entrepreneurship among high school students and the general public, and that they had a very positive view of small business compared with large corporations. The results also showed that the small business owners were especially satisfied with their career choice and preferred to run their own businesses rather than work for large corporations.

The hypothetical question asked in the 2002 survey was slightly different, removing working at a corporation as the alternative choice with a more neutral option. The question stated: "Thinking about business, if you had the choice between starting your own business or working for someone else who owns a business, which would you rather do?" The results from this survey question, reported in Chapter 2, are worth repeating for comparison with the 1994 responses. In 2002, over six in ten (64%) youth and the general public stated they preferred to start their own businesses rather than work for someone else. Almost nine in ten (85%) business owners supplied the same response.

Although the questions from each time period are slightly different in wording, the responses to both questions about starting or owning a business from high school students, the general public, and small business owners are quite similar across time. Both high school students and the general public show highly positive opinions about starting a business or being a business owner. As was expected, the small business owners gave the most positive response to either question among all three groups, again indicating the high degree of satisfaction with their decision to become entrepreneurs.

An exact comparison of entrepreneurial interest comes from the question about wanting to start a business of one's own because the questions are the same (Table 7.1).[2] Slightly more than two-thirds (69%) of the high school students stated in 1994 that they wanted to start businesses of their own and slightly less than two-thirds (65%) gave the same response in 2002. The difference was slight and within the margin of sampling error, thus indicating stability in the responses of youth. For the general public, half (50%) stated they wanted to start a business in 1994 and slightly more (55%) gave the same response in 2002, a minor difference.

Table 7.1 Want to Start Own Business, 1994 and 2002[a]

	High School Students		General Public	
	1994	2002	1994	2002
Response	(n=602)	(1,010)	(600)	(607)
Yes	69%	65%	50%	55%
No	28	33	49	45
Don't know/Refused	3	1	1	1

Note: [a]"Do you think you would want to start a business of your own?"

The reasons given for why other people start businesses show some consistency over time, at least on recognition of the main reason among two of the three groups (Table 7.2). Business owners show most agreement with the reason of being your own boss. About nine in ten in 1994 (91%) and also in 2002 (89%) gave a strongly agree or agree response to that option. This reason also drew the most agreement from the general public in both years and was at about the same level as that of business owners, with almost nine in ten of the general public giving such a response each year.

High school students, by contrast, showed a more mixed view of the reasons in both years. Being your own boss was rated highest (73%) in 1994, but so was building something for the family (73%). Being your own boss was again rated highly (77%) in 2002, the same as using your skills and abilities (77%), but not quite as highly as earning lots of money (78%). The conclusion from both time periods is that youth had a more uncertain opinion about the reasons other people start their own businesses. The general public and business owners recognized the autonomy of ownership as the most important reason for why people want to start businesses.

Table 7.2 Reasons Other People Go into Business, 1994 and 2002[a]

	High School Students		General Public		Business Owners	
	1994	2002	1994	2002	1994	2002
Reasons	(n=602)	(1,010)	(600)	(607)	(204)	(403)
To earn lots of money	64%	78%	54%	69%	47%	57%
To be your own boss	73	77	88	89	91	89
To use skills and abilities	68	77	80	78	78	78
To build something for family	73	68	78	80	83	73
To overcome a challenge	48	42	55	49	58	45

Note: [a]"Using a five point scale, where 5 means you strongly agree and 1 means that you strongly disagree, do you think people go into business:" (The percentages reported in this table are the total of the strongly agree and agree responses.)

There were some changes in the percentage responses over time for the various reasons, but nothing that suggests a pattern or a trend. The one exception to this conclusion is the pecuniary motivation of earning lots of money. It showed a sizable increase in the percentages for high school students (+14), the general public (+15), and business owners (+10). This change probably reflects greater interest in material concerns or wealth-building which were given more emphasis in popular culture, the media, and society over the period of the two surveys.[3]

In 1994 and again in 2002, an open-ended question was asked of the sub-sample of high school students and the general public who stated that they were interested in starting their own businesses (Table 7.3).[4] Similar results were found in both years. Over four in ten (43% to 45%) high school students who were interested in starting a business cited being your own boss more than any other one factor as the major reason for starting a new business. About five in ten (48% to 51%) of the general public gave the same response in both years. Earning lots of money as a motivating reason was cited by two in ten or less in each group. The percentage response for this reason was about the same each year.

Table 7.3 Major Reason You Want to Start Own Business, 1994 and 2002[a]

Reasons	High School Students		General Public	
	1994	**2002**	**1994**	**2002**
	(n=415)[b]	(664)[b]	(300)[b]	(281)[b]
To be my own boss	43%	45%	51%	48%
To earn lots of money	18	20	14	18
To use my skills and abilities	7	11	6	9
To overcome a challenge	6	4	9	5
To build something for the family	6	3	7	6
To help the community/Provide jobs	11	3	5	4
Other	7	4	7	7
No specific reason	–	6	–	2
Don't know/Refused	3	4	1	1

Notes:
[a]"What is the major reason why you might want to start a business for yourself?"
[b]For YES respondents on whether you'd want to start a business of your own.

The stability of these results over time provides support for the conclusion that high school students thought earning lots of money was less important as a motivating reason when they wanted to start businesses of their own, but they considered it to be significantly more important as a motivating reason when other people wanted to start businesses. By contrast, many high school students thought the autonomy afforded by being your own boss was a prime reason for why they wanted to start their own businesses, but they had more mixed opinions about the matter when they were asked to consider the motivations of other people who wanted to start businesses. In either year, however, the results show that youth think that other people are driven by material motives whereas when they consider entrepreneurship for themselves, it is because they are primarily driven by the need for control and independence.

COMMUNITY RESPONSIBILITY

One question on the 1994 survey asked all three groups about their views on the community responsibility of business owners: "How important do you think it is for successful business owners or entrepreneurs to give something back to the community beyond providing jobs?" The three permissible responses were *very important, somewhat important,* or *not at all important.*

All three groups overwhelmingly stated that it was either very important or somewhat important. Among high school students (n=602), over two-thirds (68%) stated it was very important and less than one-third (31%) stated that it was somewhat important. The responses of the general public (n=600) were quite similar to those of high school students, with over two-thirds (68%) answering that it was very important and less than one-third (28%) saying was somewhat important. Among business owners (n=204), almost six in ten (59%) replied that it was very important and over one-third (37%) said it was somewhat important. The predominant response that was supplied by the overwhelming majority of each group was that it was *very important* for successful business owners to give something back to the community.

There is no exactly equivalent question on the 2002 survey to make a precise longitudinal comparison on this issue, but there was a similar question on that survey that provides some insights: "Using a five-point scale, where '5' is 'very important' and '1' is 'not at all important,' how important do you think it is for successful business owners or entrepreneurs to contribute something to the community beyond providing jobs or paying taxes?" The 2002 version had the minor change of adding "or paying taxes" as a qualifier at the end of the statement and uses a broader scale for the survey responses.

The survey responses from this item were provided in Chapter 3, but they are restated here for the sake of convenience (Table 7.4). As was the case in 1994, the predominant response that was supplied by about half or more of each group was very important. The percentages are less than those given as very important in 1994, but the use of a five-point rather than a three-point scale probably explains most of the difference. Some respondents who selected "important" with the five-point scale in 2002 most likely would have selected "very important" on a three-point scale when the next option was only "somewhat important." Totaling the very important (5) and important (4) responses in 2002 may overstate what would be given as answers if there was only a three-point scale, but not by a large amount. If that assumption holds, then any differences over time about the importance of the community responsibility of successful business owners would be minimal. The point of this speculation is that the opinions about giving back to the community that were stated in 1994 seem to be about the same as those expressed in 2002.[5]

Table 7.4 Importance of a Community Contribution[a]

	2002		
Response	**High School Students** (1,010)	**General Public** (607)	**Business Owners** (403)
5 Very important	49%	57%	48%
4	31	24	23
3	15	11	22
2	3	3	4
1 Not at all important	2	4	3
Don't know/Refused	1	2	1

Note: [a]"Using a five-point scale, where 5 is very important, and 1 is not at all important, how important do you think it is for successful business owners or entrepreneurs to contribute something to the community beyond providing jobs or paying taxes?"

ENTREPRENEURIAL KNOWLEDGE

Six test items were included on both the 1994 and 2002 surveys, which meant that the test scores could be compared over time. The findings from the 2002 survey showed a lack of knowledge and understanding of entrepreneurship, business, and economic concepts among young potential entrepreneurs that was troubling. The results show little change over time. In 1994, high school students, on average, correctly answered about 50% of the entrepreneurship test questions. This result is virtually the same as in 2002, when high school students, on average, correctly answered 52% of the questions, which is only a slight improvement (Table 7.5).

Table 7.5 Entrepreneurial Knowledge Questions, 1994 and 2002[a]

Score	High School Students		General Public		Business Owners	
	1994	2002	1994	2002	1994	2002
	(n=602)	(1,010)	(600)	(607)	(204)	(403)
Description of entrepreneur	70%	74%	78%	85%	89%	90%
Small business and job creation	28	31	46	55	65	70
Business survival	49	47	54	66	90	82
Example of franchise	70	63	80	85	96	95
Supply and demand	60	64	59	71	86	85
Purpose of profits	25	34	33	41	62	51
Mean	**50%**	**52%**	**58%**	**68%**	**81%**	**79%**

Note: [a]See Chapter 4 for the wording of the six test questions and the detailed responses.

Although the overall difference was negligible, the differences in the percentage correct on individual items were more pronounced. High school students scored better in the 2002 survey on four items (entrepreneur, jobs creation, supply and demand, and profits) and worse on two items (business survival and franchise). The item differences, however, are minor and most likely due to sampling error. They suggest no change or trend over time.

The survey findings show that the general public improved their knowledge scores from 1994 to 2002. The general public gave correct responses to 58% of the items in 1994 and 68% of the items in 2002, an increase of 10 percentage points in their knowledge scores. This change represents an increase from a little more than three correct responses out of six questions to more than four correct responses out of six. The item responses also showed improvement from 1994 to 2002. The general public was more correct by 12 percentage points in knowing that cash flow was the most important factor for business survival. Their understanding that supply and demand factors determine prices in a competitive market increased by 12 percentage points. A nine percentage-point improvement was found in their awareness of the contribution of small business to jobs creation. Eight percent more of the general public knew the purpose of profits in 2002 than in 1994. The general public showed a seven percentage-point improvement in their ability to supply a definition of an entrepreneur. They were more correct by five percentage points in identifying a franchise.

This increase in knowledge and skills related to entrepreneurship among the general public may be evidence that the mass media and the growth of the Internet has had an effect on general knowledge of business concepts between 1994 and 2002. It was during this period that there was an explosive growth in the use of the Internet and the information technology sector.

More people also were invested in the stock markets than had participated historically, which may have exposed these investors to more information about finance and business practices. Information available to adults through mass and media sources most likely contributed to this increased knowledge.[6]

The scores for business owners show a slight decrease by two percentage points from 1994 to 2002. This minor change, however, is most likely due to sampling error and does not reflect any substantive change in knowledge or understanding of starting a business. In either year, business owners had an average percentage correct of about 80%. As was expected, it was the highest of any group in both years surveyed.[7]

The test scores for high school students on the knowledge questions are about the same in each year, so it would be expected that their self-ratings of knowledge or understanding of starting a business should not show a drastic difference (Table 7.6). That conclusion holds. In 2002, youth rated their knowledge and understanding somewhat better than they had in 1994, but the change was minor. In the earlier interview, 86% of youth rated their knowledge or understanding as fair, poor, or very poor compared with 77% in 2002. At the other end of the spectrum, 13% of teenagers described their knowledge and understanding of starting and managing a business as good or excellent in 1994, but 23% did so in 2002. This latter change may appear to be substantial, but the change starts from a low base and in either year only a minority of students expressed great confidence in their entrepreneurial knowledge. In addition, their actual performance on the entrepreneurship test essentially was the same in both years, so any improvement in their self-assessments would not be well founded and may simply reflect increased interest, desire, or exposure to business-related ideas.

Table 7.6 Knowledge of Starting a Business, 1994 and 2002[a]

	High School Students		General Public	
	1994	2002	1994	2002
Response	(n=602)	(1,010)	(600)	(607)
5 Excellent	4%	5%	11%	15%
4	9	18	14	19
3	42	47	34	34
2	30	22	19	16
1 Very poor	14	8	21	15
Don't know/Refused	0	0	1	—

Note: [a]"aFor high school students and the general public the question was: "Using a five-point scale, where 5 is excellent, and 1 is very poor, how would you describe your knowledge and understanding of starting and managing a business?"

Members of the general public had more reason to assess themselves higher on the entrepreneurial knowledge and understanding scale in 2002 since their performance on the entrepreneurship and business management items actually improved over this period. Like high school students, they rated themselves as good or excellent more often in 2002. The increase was from one-fourth (25%) to one-third (34%). At the other extreme, 74% of the general public rated itself as fair to very poor in its entrepreneurial knowledge in 1994, but only 65% rated themselves that low in 2002.[8]

MARKETS AND GOVERNMENT

In the 1994 study, all three groups were asked: "If the supply of new houses was reduced by a shortage of lumber, do you think that the government should prohibit construction companies from raising prices on new houses?" In 2002, almost the same question was asked: "If a shortage of lumber increased the cost of building houses, do you think the government should prohibit construction companies from raising prices on new houses?" The reason for the change was to make the question more direct and easier to understand.

In 1994, almost six in ten (57%) of youth said that the government should prohibit these construction companies from raising their prices (Table 7.7) and only a minority (41%) were opposed to the intervention by government in this market. The response of the general public was more evenly divided, with about half (49%) supporting price controls and about half (47%) against. A minority (23%) of business owners supported government intervention while the great majority (77%) opposed them.

Table 7.7 Government Should Prohibit Price Increases, 1994 and 2002[a]

	High School Students		General Public		Business Owners	
	1994	2002	1994	2002	1994	2002
Response	(n=602)	(1,010)	(600)	(607)	(204)	(403)
Yes, prohibit	57%	38%	49%	34%	23%	16%
No, do not prohibit	41	61	47	63	77	80
Don't know/Refused	2	1	4	3	0	4

Note: [a]1994 question: "If the supply of new houses was reduced by a shortage of lumber, do you think that the government should prohibit construction companies from raising prices on new houses?" 2002 question: "If a shortage of lumber increased the cost of building houses, do you think the government should prohibit construction companies from raising prices on new houses?"

The same pattern of responses in 1994 was expected to be the same in 2002, but the results showed a dramatic inversion. Among high school students, over six in ten (61%) answered this question by saying they were opposed to government intervention to control prices. A large majority (63%) of the general public also was now opposed to this price intervention by government in the housing market. Among business owners, opposition to government control slightly increased from its previous high level (77%).

One explanation is that the change in wording affected responses. The modification was minor, however, and why it would make opinions more market-oriented is a puzzle. A second explanation is that knowledge about supply and demand improved somewhat among both groups (see Table 7.6), so that respondents were more aware of how markets should work. A third explanation is that a shift in the political or social climate gave less credence to government interference. Whatever the reason, the change was striking.

For high school students, these results may indicate more of an ownership mindset. In 2002, less than four in ten (38%) of teenagers were thinking like consumers, but the great majority (61%) thought more like entrepreneurs who could appreciate the need to raise prices when raw materials were in short supply. It suggests that although many high school students did not yet have the knowledge or understanding required to succeed as entrepreneurs, they were exhibiting, at least in this aspect, the necessary habits of mind.

The responses to the second question about prices suggest that any change in opinion or mindset among high school students was relatively minor (Table 7.8). The reason for the price change in the second question was because demand had increased for the product. About the same percentages in 1994 (65%) and in 2002 (61%) were opposed to a price increase. In this case, the question did not change at all from 1994 to 2002, so it may be a more reliable gauge of a change in opinion from one period to the next.

Table 7.8 Manufacturer Should Be Allowed to Raise Prices, 1994 and 2002[a]

	High School Students		General Public		Business Owners	
	1994	2002	1994	2002	1994	2002
Response	(n=602)	(1,010)	(600)	(607)	(204)	(403)
Yes, allowed to	34%	39%	36%	47%	66%	69%
No, not allowed to	65	61	62	52	33	29
Don't know/Refused	1	0	2	1	0	2

Note: [a]"Suppose a bicycle manufacturer raises the price of bikes because the demand for them has increased even though the cost of producing bikes has not increased. Do you think the manufacturer should be allowed to raise prices?"

The responses to the two questions, when considered as a set, also show some stability in the results over time, in spite of the shifts noted for the first question. High school students and the general public were more willing to accept a price increase based on an increase in the cost of production and a decrease in supply than they were willing to accept a price increase based on an increase in demand. The likely reason for the split in opinion on the two questions may be due to the perceived justification for the price increase. It may appear to high school students and the general public that in the second case the manufacturer was taking advantage of consumers and was not being fair to the consumer by raising prices, whereas in the first case the rationale for the price increase was more justified because it was due to a known increase in the cost of production. The findings from this second question indicate that high school students are far from developing an owner mindset or market orientation that is exhibited by most entrepreneurs. This conclusion is more consistent with the findings about the low level of entrepreneurial knowledge among youth than are the findings from the first question on prices.

One issue for which there was a substantial change in the opinions of all three groups from 1994 to 2002 was on government regulation of business. The study asked one question on this topic to provide a broad assessment of whether general views of government regulation of high school students, or the general public, were similar to those of most entrepreneurs. The question asked the respondents whether they thought there was too much, too little, or about the right amount of government regulation of business.

The results show that far fewer respondents in each group thought that there was too much government regulation of business (Table 7.9). The percentages giving this response dropped from 1994 to 2002 among high school students (–10), the general public (–10), and most surprisingly and more sharply among business owners (–19). The change in opinion, however, did not shift to any significant degree in the opposite direction of thinking that there was too little government regulation. The percentages supplying this response increased slightly for the general public (+2) and business owners (+5), but also fell for high school students (–5). Most of the change in opinion was a movement from the response that there was too much government regulation to the response that there was about the right amount of regulation. The percentages giving this more neutral response increased among high school students (+16), the general public (+9), and business owners (+11). Thus the shift in opinion over time clearly indicates that all three groups were now more neutral in their opinions about government regulation of business whereas in the past more individuals in all three groups had been more opposed to government regulation of business.

Table 7.9 Government Regulation of Business, 1994 and 2002[a]

Response	High School Students		General Public		Business Owners	
	1994	2002	1994	2002	1994	2002
	(n=602)	(1,010)	(600)	(607)	(204)	(403)
Too much government regulation	32%	22%	60%	50%	75%	56%
Too little government regulation	15	10	10	12	2	7
About the right amount of government regulation	50	66	25	34	21	32
Don't know/Refused	3	2	5	5	1	5

Note: [a]"Thinking about government regulation of business, do you think there is:"

The most likely explanation for the shift has to do with the unethical business practices that received major national attention in the several years prior to the fall, 2002, survey. During that period there were major national news, political attention, and legal actions that focused on the decline and eventual bankruptcy of Enron and corporate scandals at WorldCom and Global Crossings. These national events led to lawsuits, stricter regulatory enforcement by government agencies, and eventual passage of the Sarbanes–Oxley legislation requiring more scrutiny and oversight of business practices and boards of directors. The business developments and legal actions most likely had the effect of shifting some opinions among all three groups from being opposed to more government regulation to more thinking that government regulation of business was necessary and about right.

In either survey year, however, the results show that the majority of business owners thought there was too much government regulation of business, and to a lesser degree, a majority of the general public also thought that there was too much government regulation. Although the size of these majorities diminished for each group from 1994 to 2002, the majority view in both groups still was that there was too much government regulation.

Among high school students, by contrast, the majority in either survey year were more likely to state that government regulation of business was about right. In 1994, this percentage of youth (50%) was twice as high as the percentage of business owners (21%). In 2002, this percentage (66%) of youth also was twice as high as the percentage of business owners (32%). In essence, the difference of opinions between high school students and business owners in either survey year remained the same and appears to be relatively constant in spite of any general change in such opinions over time. In 1994, most high school students did not exhibit an owner mindset about government regulation of business, nor did they exhibit one in 2002.

A question about government taxation of business also was asked in both survey years, so it too can be used to assess the entrepreneurial mentality of youth. As was the case with the regulation item, the taxation question was a general one and sought to find if youth thought that most businesses were overtaxed, undertaxed, or taxed the right amount. The purpose of the question was to compare the views of high school students, the general public, and business owners on this issue. The opinions of business owners were the basis for assessing the degree to which high school students and the general public thought more like owners on this issue and whether those opinions had changed over time.

Unlike the regulation issue, which had shown a major shift over the eight-year period, there was surprising little movement in opinions about business taxation among all three groups (Table 7.10). Almost seven in ten (69%) business owners stated that businesses were overtaxed in 1994 and in 2002 just over seven in ten (71%) stated that businesses were overtaxed. A negligible fraction (4%) of business owners in either year stated that businesses were undertaxed. A quarter or less (25% to 22%) of business owners answered that businesses were taxed about the right amount in either year. The clear opinion of owners about business taxes is that they are too high, and this opinion has not changed over time.

Youth were split on the tax question, but more so in 2002 than in 1994. Almost half (48%) of high school students answered that they thought that businesses were overtaxed in 1994, and a slightly smaller percentage (46%) gave the same reply in 2002. Fewer high school youth stated that businesses were undertaxed in 2002 (9%) than in 1994 (13%), but the change was minor. If there was any change among youth over time, it was to the position that businesses were taxed the right amount with an increase of seven percentage points from 1994 (34%) to 2002 (41%).

Table 7.10 Views of Taxation, 1994 and 2002[a]

	High School Students		General Public		Business Owners	
	1994	**2002**	**1994**	**2002**	**1994**	**2002**
Response	(n=602)	(1,010)	(600)	(607)	(204)	(403)
Overtaxed	48%	46%	48%	46%	69%	71%
Undertaxed	13	9	19	15	4	4
Taxed about the right amount	34	41	26	32	25	22
Don't know/Refused	5	4	7	7	1	3

Note: [a]"Thinking about taxes, do you think that most businesses are:"

The opinions of the general public were quite similar to those of high school students in both years. Almost half (49%) of the general public said that businesses were overtaxed in 1994, and, as was the case with high school students, a slightly smaller percentage (46%) supplied the same answer in 2002. About one-third (32%) of the general public thought that businesses were taxed about the right amount, which is an increase from over about a quarter (26%) who gave the same response in 1994. A small percentage of the general public in both 1994 and 2002 stated that businesses were undertaxed.

For either survey year, the results show that high school students and business owners differed substantially in their opinions about taxation. Similar differences are found between the business owners and the general public. Business owners are much more likely than high school students, or the general public, to state that businesses are overtaxed, and those differences remain relatively constant based on the evidence from the recent and prior surveys of all three groups. Although the general sentiment expressed by high school students and the general public is that businesses are overtaxed, that view is not a majority position of either group, whereas it clearly was the majority position of business owners. This conclusion about business taxation holds for either year, indicating that the findings for 2002 are not unique to that year among the groups surveyed.

ENTREPRENEURSHIP EDUCATION

The survey responses from 1994 and 2002 showed that high school students lack knowledge of entrepreneurship (see Table 7.5). The average percentage correct on the knowledge test was 50% in 1994 and 52% in 2002. Most students also self-rated their knowledge and understanding as being deficient (see Table 7.6). In 1994, 86% of high school students gave themselves a fair to very poor rating on their knowledge of entrepreneurship. This percentage dropped to 77% in 2002, but the high level still indicates that most youth lack confidence in their entrepreneurial knowledge.

The knowledge scores and self-ratings from either year suggest that most youth were not educated for entrepreneurship. One likely reason for these outcomes is that many high school students failed to receive any direct instruction in entrepreneurship, business, economics, or related subjects in school. A question on coursework was included in the surveys in both years. It asked the interviewees to indicate whether they had taken a high school course in business or entrepreneurship, a course in economics, or a course in personal finance or consumer economics (Table 7.11).

Table 7.11 Courses Taken in High School, 1994 and 2002[a]

	High School Students		General Public		Business Owners	
	1994	2002	1994	2002	1994	2002
Response	(n=602)	(1,010)	(564)[b]	(587)[b]	(204)[b]	(399)[b]
A course in economics	35%	39%	39%	46%	38%	34%
A course in personal finance or consumer economics	35	27	39	29	38	22
A course in business or entrepreneurship	27	30	25	27	26	17

Notes:
[a]"In high school, have you taken or are you currently taking:"
[b]For respondents who attended high school.

In 1994, less than three in ten (27%) high school students reported taking a course in either business or entrepreneurship. In 2002, the number increased slightly to three in ten (30%) in 2002. The results for either year demonstrate that the vast majority (73% to 70%) of youth did not participate in the type of course instruction that would give them basic knowledge or skills to prepare for the world of business and entrepreneurship. More high school students took an economics course in 2002 (39%) than in 1994 (35%), but the percentage was still less than four in ten, so the extent of that coursework remained relatively the same for this foundation subject for entrepreneurship. In the case of personal finance or consumer economics, a subject covering similar economic or financial decisions to those made by entrepreneurs, such coursework declined somewhat from 1994 (35%) to 2002 (27%) among high school students.

Nothing in the course-taking data indicates that there should be any reason to expect any improvement in high school student knowledge of entrepreneurship or economics over the intervening years. The lack of widespread instruction in core subjects related to entrepreneurship simply supplies one likely reason why high school youth showed only limited knowledge and understanding of entrepreneurship and related concepts and gave themselves relatively low self-ratings in these areas in both years.

A similar conclusion about the coursework and knowledge relationship can be drawn from the general public based on their reported course instruction in the above subjects in high school. That course instruction did not change substantially from 1994 to 2002. There was a relatively minor improvement in the percentages taking economics, which may explain the minor improvement in the knowledge scores of the general public from 1994 to 2002 because knowledge of economics was included in that test.

The responses of business owners showed a slight downward trend across all three types of courses from one time period to the other. In either survey year, however, only a minority of the business owners, while in high school, took courses in business or entrepreneurship, economics, or personal finance, so such education does not appear to be a prime source of preparation for this group. They were more likely to obtain the knowledge and understanding for starting a business from other sources, such as higher education, job training, or life experiences because so little education would have been provided to them in high school. This situation has not changed over time.

About three-fourths of owners of small businesses attended a college or university as indicated in both the 1994 and 2002 surveys. Most of these business owners received some education that prepared them for entrepreneurship in these institutions of higher education (Table 7.12). This education came from courses in small business or entrepreneurship, other business courses, or in economics courses. The results for the two survey years show a slight decrease in such course-taking over the period but there is no substantive change that would suggest that the results reported for 2002 are odd. The same basic conclusion applies to the findings for the general public for those members of the general public who attended a college or university.

Table 7.12 Courses Taken in College, 1994 and 2002[a]

Response	General Public		Business Owners	
	1994	**2002**	**1994**	**2002**
	$(272)^b$	$(311)^b$	$(164)^b$	$(301)^b$
A course in economics	47%	50%	68%	62%
A course in business or entrepreneurship	24	17	37	27
Other business courses (such as accounting, business law, finance, management, and marketing)	51	58	72	61

Notes:
[a]"In college, did you take:"
[b]For respondents who attended college.

A final comparison of the data over time can be made with the opinions of all three groups about the importance of teaching about entrepreneurship and starting a business in the schools. Given the possible range of opinion on the matter, the respondents were asked to rate their views on the importance of schools to provide entrepreneurship education rather than give simply a yes or no response. The scale ranged from "1" to "5," where a "5" denoted "very important" and "1" was "not at all important."

What is quite remarkable is that the ratings supplied by high school students in both 1994 and 2002 are almost exactly the same (Table 7.13). Almost five in ten high school students in 1994 and 2002 responded that it was very important for the nation's schools to teach students about entrepreneurship and starting a business. Over three in ten in 1994 and 2002 stated that it was important for the nation's schools to teach students about entrepreneurship and starting a business. Only a small minority (16% or 19%) of high school students in either year gave an uncertain or negative response.

Table 7.13 Importance to Teach Entrepreneurship, 1994 and 2002[a]

Response	High School Students		General Public		Business Owners	
	1994	2002	1994	2002	1994	2002
	(n=602)	(1,010)	(600)	(607)	(204)	(403)
5 Very important	48%	49%	60%	59%	61%	73%
4	36	32	22	22	20	15
3	14	14	13	14	16	7
2	1	3	2	2	3	2
1 Not at all important	1	2	3	3	0	2
Don't know/Refused	0	0	1	–	0	1

Note: [a]"Using a five-point scale, where 5 is very important, and 1 is not at all important, how important is it for our nation's schools to teach students about entrepreneurship and starting a business?"

The views of the general public also were essentially the same in 1994 and 2002, but the general public was even more supportive of the need for entrepreneurship education than were high school students. About six in ten of the general public in 1994 and 2002 thought that it was very important for the nation's schools to teach about entrepreneurship and starting a business. Over two in ten of the general public surveyed in each year thought it was important to provide such education. Less than two in ten of the general public queried in 1994 and 2002 were uncertain about the need or had a negative opinion of such education. Clearly, there was consistent support expressed over time for providing entrepreneurship education in the schools.

If there was any major change over the years in the opinions expressed by each of the three groups about the importance of teaching about entrepreneurship and starting a business in the nation's schools, it was to be found among business owners. In 1994, 61% of business owners stated that it was very important that the nation's schools should teach more about entrepreneurship and starting a business. By 2002, the percentage increased to 73%. The increase came from respondents who had previously thought it was only important (–5%) or who were uncertain (–8%). The 2002 findings reveal that there was near unanimity among business owners about entrepreneurship education for youth.

The explanation for this shift in opinion among business owners is difficult to identify, but it is likely due to more recognition of the general benefits of entrepreneurship for society. From 1994 to 2002 there was greater emphasis on, and study of, the value of entrepreneurship and the contributions it can make to economic growth and the national economy, to community development and philanthropy, and to social mobility and economic advancement.[9] Such activity would have influenced the thinking of business owners and may explain why they became stronger advocates of entrepreneurship education for youth over the eight years.

MAJOR FINDINGS

The general conclusion to be drawn from all the longitudinal comparisons is that the responses of high school students, the general public, and business owners to most of the questions asked in the 2002 survey are often quite similar to the responses to the same questions in 1994. Where there are changes, they are relatively minor or inconsequential. In a few cases, there are significant changes, but they are in the expected direction, and events during the period largely explain the shift in opinions. The major point from the longitudinal analysis is that the 2002 survey results are not unique to that year or odd in any way. They are completely consistent with what was found in survey work conducted in prior years using the same or similar questions. Therefore, the many interpretations that were drawn from the 2002 findings, and reported in the five previous chapters in this book, have more general applicability and validity beyond the specific year of the survey.

The remainder of the chapter summarizes the most important or major findings from the 2002 survey. It presents basic conclusions about the entrepreneurial interest of high school students, their attitudes toward community, their knowledge of entrepreneurship and views of markets and government, the potential obstacles youth face in starting businesses, and what they think the educational system can do to help them. Although the summary may restate what has been reported already in this chapter and the ones before, it provides a concise overview of the key results that should be useful for considering the implications and extrapolations of the final chapter.

1. Youth show great interest in entrepreneurship.

The obstacles to business ownership, combined with the continued lack of education in this area, and especially the recent negative media images of greedy "business types," would be expected to erode teenagers' interest in entrepreneurship. The interview data, however, belied any initial pessimistic expectations about the desire for entrepreneurship. They revealed a high level of interest among U.S. high school students.

This great interest was observed and demonstrated in four ways. First, high school students were asked to make a hypothetical choice between working for another person and working for themselves. By a substantial majority (65%), high school students said they would prefer to work for themselves. Second, in a more direct question, they were asked if they wanted to start a business of their own. Again, about two-thirds responded in the affirmative. Third, they were probed to find out how likely it was that they would act on an idea to start a business. About half reported they were likely or very likely to initiate their own venture. Fourth, small business owners were asked when they had first become interested in going into business for themselves. One in five business owners said the first thoughts of starting their own ventures occurred to them when they were less than 20 years old. Another 20% developed this idea when they were between 20–24 years old, and almost 30% started to think about undertaking a business enterprise when they were 25–30 years old. These retrospective responses also probably apply to the current generation and support a trend of ongoing interest in potential entrepreneurship among young people.

An important part of the story of entrepreneurial interest is the difference between groups of young people. Males and females showed comparable levels of interest, although females were slightly less interested, especially when these young women were asked directly whether they would start a business. More striking was the higher proportion of entrepreneurial interest among minority youth compared to white youth. Over three-fourths (77%) of African American youth said they would prefer working for themselves and almost as many (75%) said they wanted to start a business. Likewise, three-fourths (75%) of Hispanic youth reported they would prefer to start their own businesses than to work for someone else, and 70% stated their intent to do so. These preferences were high compared to whites, who only 60% of the time answered that they would prefer to work for themselves and 63% of the time reported wanting to start businesses of their own. African Americans (67%) and Hispanics (64%) also stated more frequently than whites (50%) that they were likely or very likely to act on an entrepreneurial idea. This great interest among minority youth became a theme in the study.

2. Youth want to achieve economic autonomy by being business owners.

There are many reasons high school students might want to start businesses. For those who view young people as dangerously susceptible to media-generated ideas of get-rich-quick schemes, it may come as a surprise that the primary reason that high school students gave by a large margin for wanting to start their own businesses was not to "earn lots of money," but to "be their own boss." This finding squared with the responses of members of the public who wanted to start their own businesses. Existing small business owners also reported for themselves similar motivations for going into business.

Not only were they self-motivated by the idea of economic autonomy, but high school students' general views about business ownership also reflected this idea as well, although to a lesser extent. Youth were asked the reasons they thought *others* might be interested in starting their own ventures, and about half (52%) reported that others start businesses for reasons of economic independence. About the same proportion (54%) of high school students said they thought others started businesses to "earn lots of money," a result that may express the belief among young people that entrepreneurship does increase the potential of achieving affluence. Nevertheless, the goal of independence, combined with other aims such as family concerns, using skills, or meeting challenges, far outweighed earning money as motivations.

Economic autonomy, therefore, emerged as another major theme in this book. Respondents from all three groups may have been keenly aware of the motivational power of wanting to be one's own boss. This attitude may reflect individual character: many Americans may want to strike out on their own and use their own wits and strengths to achieve something they could attribute to their personal efforts and abilities. The desire to be one's own boss and to initiate a venture also may reflect a growing knowledge – either intuitive or conscious – of the economic forces such as technological change, globalization of markets, and increased business competition that have created turmoil in the U.S. economy over the past few decades. Many Americans may perceive that business ownership holds the best promise for social mobility and a more economically self-sufficient future.

3. Youth want to contribute to communities and be social entrepreneurs.

Several related findings led to the conclusion that the philanthropic and communal spirit is alive and thriving among this nation's youth, and that this spirit is concomitant with young people's desires to become entrepreneurs. The manifestation of such dual interest is what we have identified as an entrepreneurial spirit combined with the community or social mindset.

The most striking evidence of this communal spirit is the proportion of high school students (about two-thirds) who want both to start their own businesses, as discussed above in the first finding, *and* to start non-profit or philanthropic organizations. Considering that each group comprises greater than half of the sample, there must be a minimum overlap of approximately 40%, and the overlap could well be considerably higher. At least two in every five high school students apparently would like both to start a charitable organization *and* a business.

As discussed in Chapter 3, these seemingly dissonant aspirations might represent a "pipedream" for some and for others may generate inertia-causing cognitive dissonance. For many others, however, the entrepreneurial and communal spirits may be the raw materials that will lead them to join the growing ranks of the *new social entrepreneurs*. A quality education for entrepreneurship could serve as a catalyst to combine these seemingly disparate elements into an economically potent solution. Such a catalytic educational initiative would be aimed at the interests and needs of young people highlighted in this book, and it would include a focus on social entrepreneurship: the option of initiating not-for-profit or social agenda-driven ventures as well as purely for-profit ventures. It also would emphasize business enterprises that contribute actively to their communities in both economic and non-economic ways.

The communal spirit not only was evident in young people's desires to start philanthropic organizations, but was apparent when they were asked how important it was for successful entrepreneurs to contribute something to the community in addition to providing jobs and paying taxes. About half of high school students said these kinds of contributions were very important. This proportion was slightly less than that among the general public (57%), but virtually identical to that of business owners. African American students indicated it was very important even more often – 65% of the time.

Though they thought businesses should give back to the community in a variety of economic and non-economic ways, when asked how businesses do contribute to the economy, only 17% of the responses that were supplied listed philanthropic contributions such as charitable donations and public service. When young people did recognize businesses' non-economic contributions, many attributed these contributions to self-interest for business survival. For example, many youth reported that they thought a major reason a business owner might contribute to the community was to promote his or her business. At the same time, however, half of the respondents said "wanting to help" was a major reason a business owner might contribute to the community, and about one-third said that business owners contribute to the community because they personally believe in voluntary giving.

4. Youth lack essential knowledge and skills to be entrepreneurial in their work or to become entrepreneurs.

Despite their interest in becoming entrepreneurs, high school students in general face a barrier in their lack of entrepreneurial skills, understanding of business management, and economic knowledge. On six entrepreneurial knowledge questions that were included as a short test in the survey, high school students correctly answered just over half the questions, on average. These results suggest that there were substantial gaps in the knowledge of high school students on basic questions of entrepreneurship and business.

Young people do have a grasp of some basic business management and economic concepts. By and large, they could define the term "entrepreneur," and six in ten could correctly identify a franchise. Further, almost two-thirds knew that supply and demand determine prices. Only a third, however, knew that small businesses create most of the jobs in the U.S. economy, and less than half knew that cash flow was the most important factor in business survival. Most high school students misunderstood the role of profit in rewarding entrepreneurs for marshaling resources and sustaining risk to produce products and services customers want to buy. The somewhat good news is that, compared to earlier results, the data from the latest interviews did not show the knowledge level of high school students to have decreased.

The poor showing on this short entrepreneurship test demonstrates the scope of the problem. It is reasonable to expect responses to such basic test questions to be correct much more than half of the time if high school students are to become a more powerful contributing factor to the engine of economic growth. Perhaps just as interesting as measuring the dimension of the educational challenge is the evidence that high school students are aware of their own ignorance. Three-quarters of these youth rated themselves fair to poor on their level of entrepreneurial knowledge.

5. Youth often view markets and government in ways that inhibit entrepreneurship and are inconsistent with an owner perspective.

Business owners were found to have developed a distinctive attitude toward government, markets, and taxation that appeared to be based on their first-hand experiences with regulatory compliance and paying taxes. This attitude can be summed up as wariness of government intervention in the natural flow of markets and a general aversion to regulation and taxation that excessively impede a business's ability to compete and grow. The results, based on interviews with owners of small businesses, show this attitude so sufficiently widespread that it can be reasonably characterized as an "ownership mentality" or entrepreneurial mindset. As a way of measuring the extent to which young people, especially aspiring future entrepreneurs, shared this worldview, high school students were asked a number of questions related to markets, regulation, and taxation. The extent that these teenagers' attitudes diverged from those of business owners indicated that many teenagers had not developed an ownership mindset about government and markets.

What was found was not surprising given the differences in age, experience, and mindsets. When asked about the support for price controls, high school students appeared to make judgments based on a consumer notion of fairness, rather than on an appreciation of how markets respond to decreased supply and increased demand in such a way as to preserve the business owner's incentives to continue producing its products and services and "stay in the market." Although many high school students were opposed to government intervention in pricing that prohibited business owners from recouping increased costs of production, they were not opposed to and in fact supported price controls that prohibit businesses from adapting to increased demand. In the area of price controls, then, young people did not exhibit an ownership mentality or a real de facto knowledge of how markets work.

The overlap between entrepreneurs' and high school students' perceptions of government regulation was also measured. Over half of the small business owners thought the government imposed too many regulations on businesses, whereas two-thirds of high school students estimated that government regulation was about right. It is clear that high school students did not share business owners' concerns about over-regulation even though they aspire to be business owners themselves. High school students and business owners also failed to see eye to eye on the issue of taxes. A large majority of business owners felt overtaxed, whereas most high school students believed that businesses were either taxed about the right amount or even undertaxed.

In exploring the fit between the mentality of the aspiring teenage entrepreneur and the existing business owner, therefore, the survey data showed that attitudes toward government, markets, regulation, and taxes among high school students did not closely match those of business owners. Because high school students appeared to lack both an understanding of markets and an ownership mentality, this combination constitutes another barrier facing young future entrepreneurs.

6. Youth consider entrepreneurship education to be an essential and vital step for achieving their aspirations of becoming an entrepreneur.

Given that high school students have a high degree of interest in entrepreneurship, but that their knowledge base is so weak that it constitutes a real barrier to achieving this goal, the natural next question was to inquire what public schools are doing to help young people acquire the knowledge and skills necessary to become entrepreneurs and whether public high schools are the appropriate avenue for additional instruction in this area. Interview results showed that less than half of any group (high school students, members of the general public, and business owners) had taken any course related to economics, and much smaller percentages had taken courses in business management, or entrepreneurship, in high school. The irony of this lack of coursework is that seven in ten high school students claimed an interest in learning more about entrepreneurship.

Business owners generally had acquired their business-related instruction in a college or university, at least as reported by those business owners who attended an institution of higher education. Perhaps the college or university setting is the most appropriate forum for classes that teach the skills and knowledge needed to become a business owner or a founder of a not-for-profit venture if a person goes to a college or university. A high school education that prepares youth for entrepreneurship might be important for all students regardless of whether they attend college. To investigate this issue, all three groups were asked in the survey whether teaching entrepreneurship in high school was desirable and appropriate.

It was expected high school students would want their entrepreneurship instruction in their current schools and this expectation was met. Over eight in ten (81%) high school students stated that it was important or very important for the nation's schools to teach students about entrepreneurship and starting a business. It was anticipated that the general public, as the constituency and "bankrollers" for the nation's schools, might be less enthusiastic and supportive of entrepreneurship education. The opposite was true: an identical proportion of over eight in ten (81%) of the general public rated the importance of providing entrepreneurship education as important or very important. Furthermore, if both high school students themselves and members of the general public saw value in public high schools providing entrepreneurship education, business owners were even more strongly disposed to valuing this proposition. Almost nine in ten (88%) business owners rated the desirability of the nation's schools teaching students about entrepreneurship and starting a business as important or very important, indicating the strong support they gave to entrepreneurship education for all high school students.

Thus, there are strong arguments for placing entrepreneurship education in high school. High school students are intent at some point in the future on becoming their own bosses, interested in the subject, and willing to devote time to its study. Furthermore, high school students, members of the general public, and current small business owners all support this proposition.

7. Entrepreneurship and entrepreneurship education are of particular value to minority youth.

The views of minority youth – African Americans and Hispanics – were distinguishable from white youth along several dimensions in the survey findings. Both of these minority groups expressed greater interest and intent than whites in working for themselves and wanting to start their own businesses. Compared to whites, they more often reported they were likely or very likely to initiate their own ventures, and they were less concerned with risk as a reason not to start a business.

Other areas of similarity between African American and Hispanic youth – and of diversion from white high school students – included a desire to start charitable organizations and the importance of schools teaching more about entrepreneurship. White youth expressed less interest in learning more about entrepreneurship (63%) compared with African American youth (82%) and Hispanic youth (71%). In terms of the importance attributed to schools teaching more about entrepreneurship, African American and Hispanic youth more often than white youth answered that it was important to do so. Interestingly, the pattern of answers to the questions designed to gauge an entrepreneurial mindset also was similar for African American and Hispanic youth. Both of these groups were more likely to support price controls than were white youth.

African American and Hispanic students, however, did not constitute a homogeneous group on all questions. In several interesting ways, the two groups diverged. In entrepreneurial knowledge, whereas African American and white youth had similar scores on the short entrepreneurship test (52% or 53% correct), Hispanic youth displayed much less knowledge (with an average score of only 44% correct). Also, although Hispanic youth were more interested in starting charitable organizations than were white youth, they were less interested compared to African American youth. African American youth also more frequently than Hispanic youth indicated that it was important for business owners to contribute something to the community in addition to paying taxes and creating jobs. For African American youth, the communalist spirit was interrelated strongly with the entrepreneurial spirit. In addition, whereas white and Hispanic youth exhibited similar patterns of course-taking in high school, African American high school students more often participated in entrepreneurship-related instruction including courses in economics, business management, and personal finance. They also participated more commonly in extracurricular or community programs.

This extraordinary interest in initiating their own ventures, combined with above average rates of participation in economics and business management classes, and with a strong belief that schools should be providing more entrepreneurship-related instruction portends the success of increased programs in entrepreneurship education for African American high school students. Hispanic youth also displayed both interest in entrepreneurship and a need for more education opportunities.

On average, African American and Hispanic high school students in the United States come from families that earn less than white families. This demographic fact alone suggests that policies designed to redress income disparity are necessary and desirable on general economic growth and social justice grounds. Further contributing to the case for entrepreneurship education are the facts that African American and Hispanic high school students show an interest in entrepreneurship, a need for business management and economics education, and also express the belief that it is the role of the schools to provide this type of educational programming.

NOTES

1. See Walstad (1994), Walstad and Kourilsky (1996), and Walstad and Kourilsky (1999) for more information on the 1994 survey and results. The 1994 national sample of owners of small businesses included some individuals who were managers of the firms and not the owners. The sample was not split into two groups because of its small size and because the views of owners and managers were quite similar on all the survey items. The views of the owners also dominated the overall responses because they were 70% of the sample. To simplify the reporting, this group will be referred to as small business owners.
2. The only difference in the two questions was that in 2002, the respondents were given the option of stating whether they had "already started" their own business and not just yes or no. That difference did not affect the responses of high school students because there were so few in that category. To make a strict comparison between the two surveys for this table, the 7% of the general public who answered "already started" in 2002 were included in the "yes" category for 2002, which is how the issue was handled in the 1994 survey.
3. The evidence to support this assertion can be found in the number of books that have focused on wealth creation and becoming rich. Examples of major best sellers that were published during the period are *The Millionaire Next Door* (Stanley and Danko 1996), *Rich Dad Poor Dad* (Kiyosaki and Lechter 1997), and *The Road to Wealth* (Orman 2001).

4. No comparison could be made with business owners because the question was only asked of this group in 2002 (Table 2.6) and not in 1994.

5. There are no other questions on the 1994 survey related to community responsibility or philanthropy. A survey was conducted in 1996 of youth and young adults aged 14 to 39. The findings from that survey on such issues as economic or philanthropic contributions to the community, whether business owners make sufficient contributions, the reasons for contributing, and ways to contribute are discussed in a chapter in another book (Walstad and Kourilsky 1999). Although the findings are not directly comparable with the 2002 survey because of the differences in the samples, they are largely supportive of what was reported in the 2002 survey and are described in detail in Chapter 3.

6. By contrast, the entrepreneurial knowledge of high school students did not increase proportionally during this period. This outcome may be due to the different information sources and interest of high school students. Most students still receive the majority of their information and education at school and U.S. high schools did not change their curricula during the 1990s to reflect a growing interest in investing and entrepreneurship.

7. The reason that the scores for business owners were not higher is that some had more education than others, and this education factor influences scores (see Chapter 4, note 4).

8. No comparisons could be made over time about self-confidence in entrepreneurial knowledge of business owners because they were not asked that question in 1994.

9. For example, it was during this period that there was a significant increase in programs and activities conducted by the Ewing Marion Kauffman Foundation, a multi-billion dollar foundation that is devoted to advancing entrepreneurship. Many chairs of entrepreneurship were established at colleges and universities in this time. In addition, more books were published about programs or instruction for youth entrepreneurship (e.g., Kourilsky 1999; Beroff and Adams 2000).

8. Implications and Extrapolations

Following the detailed description and explanation of all the data results, it is now reasonable to take a step back and look at the results in a broader perspective. The basic purpose is not to provide a close interpretation of the findings but rather to place them in the larger context of themes, connections, or insights that emerge from the data. This chapter turns to the implications that can be drawn from the many findings reported in the book and also offers some extrapolations from the findings to guide the future development of the entrepreneur in youth.

At the outset, the organization for the chapter needs to be explained lest it be thought that drawing implications and extrapolations will lead to a presentation of a cacophony of unrelated ideas that have no unifying structure in relation to the previous material presented in the book. The chapter is organized in ways paralleling the book's five central chapters (two through six) that presented the main results from the investigation of the entrepreneurial thinking and understanding of high school students.

The first section focuses on the issue of interest in entrepreneurship and what it means for the economy in terms of economic growth, employment, and the standard of living in society. In the second section, the attention turns to the corresponding interest in giving back to the community and discusses how such interest can be directed or channeled into social entrepreneurship. The third section presents what entrepreneurial knowledge and skills should be taught to all youth before they graduate from or leave high school. For the fourth section, the discussion switches to markets and government and the development of an ownership mindset. The fifth, and final, section returns to the issue of education that was discussed throughout the book and explains the rationale for why entrepreneurship education should be included in the school curriculum for all youth. Of course, throughout the chapter the longitudinal perspective will be cited as needed.

ENTREPRENEURIAL INTEREST AND THE ECONOMY

The contribution of small businesses to the national economy and to the economies of each of the fifty states is substantial. The U.S. Small Business Administration (SBA) asserts that small businesses are central to the economy and enumerates the many contributions made by small businesses. The SBA states that small businesses: (1) account for 99.7% of all employers in the United States; (2) contribute more than 50% of the non-farm private gross domestic product (GDP) in the nation; (3) employ 50.1% of non-farm workers in the private sector; (4) create 65% or more of the net new jobs in the United States; and (5) represent 97% of U.S. exporters and produce 26% of all export value.[1]

The reason for focusing on small business is that entrepreneurship underlies the formation of new businesses. It is the foundation for innovation and technological change in the economy because it introduces new products or processes. It creates new enterprises, and also entire new markets, from overlooked or undiscovered opportunities or new technologies. Some of these enterprises succeed and become quite profitable for long periods of time while others have a short life, fail, and disappear from the economic landscape. Despite this churning in the economy, with new firms starting and other firms dying, the net contributions to employment and economic growth from start-up firms are significant and important for both the short-term and long-term health and dynamism of an economy.

Such contributions from entrepreneurship to an economy have been identified, described, and studied by many economists over the years.[2] One recent econometric study investigated the effects of small business on economic growth in states in the 1988–2002 period. It quantified the effects of small business activity and found that the "births" of small business firms are prime determinants of gross state product, employment, and state personal income. By contrast, the "death" of small business establishments significantly reduced state economic growth. The effects of these births and deaths on a state's economy are essentially the same, so for economic growth to increase in a state, the rate of births needs to exceed the rate of deaths.[3] In essence, entrepreneurship is vital to the economic health of states.

Although entrepreneurship has many benefits for the national economy and the states' economies, tapping into that prime contributor to innovation and growth is not without its challenges. The culture, institutions, and history of communities, states, and nations may influence the willingness of people to become entrepreneurs and start new firms. Such factors also may determine whether people adopt an entrepreneurial spirit to finding solutions to problems regardless of where they work or what they do even if they are not business owners. It is this entrepreneurial spirit or culture that must be nourished and supported for a society to realize its full potential for achieving the economic or social benefits that come from entrepreneurship.[4]

In this regard, interest in entrepreneurship among youth and the provision of a high-quality education in entrepreneurship for youth becomes critical for the national economy and the states' economies. Youth will be the source of the next generation of entrepreneurs and create the new firms that fuel economic growth, a rise in incomes, and more employment. Youth also will influence and be the future source for the more entrepreneurial thinking in any line of work or activity that they choose to do, even if it does not involve starting a new business venture.

What was found in this study was that over six in ten (65%) of high school students said they wanted to start their own businesses. This interest also has been relatively stable over time. Of this interested group, over five in ten (54%) said they were either very likely (19%) or likely (35%) to start their own businesses. What these percentages mean is that over one-third (35%) of high school students wanted to start businesses of their own *and* stated they were either very likely or likely to do so. These results show a great potential pool of future entrepreneurs (35,000 students for every 100,000 students). This sizable pool could become a major source for increased innovation, greater employment, more income, and a rise in productivity in the U.S. economy. If more youth could be encouraged, through better education and preparation, to consider the path of entrepreneurship at some point over their working lives and careers, then this change would confer these significant economic and social benefits to the nation and the states.

An extrapolation is worthwhile to indicate how little change would be needed to realize some of these benefits. A study of entrepreneurial activity in 2005 found that only 0.29% of the adults (aged 20–64), or 290 out of every 100,000 adults, created new businesses each month.[5] Over the 1996 to 2005 period, this percentage had shown little variation, from a low of 0.29 to a high of 0.32%. Given these findings, all it would take is another 40 adults per month to start businesses to shift the percentages beyond the high point of its past range to a new higher level of 0.33%.

Those few additional adults, and certainly more, would be willing to start new businesses and act on their entrepreneurial inclinations, if as youth they received more education about entrepreneurship. If more high school students were educated with the basic knowledge and skills to start new firms, and also felt confident in their entrepreneurial abilities, they would likely start their own businesses at some point in their lives as adults. As has been shown, the thought of becoming an entrepreneur often comes early in life even if the act of becoming one comes later in life.[6]

GIVING BACK AND SOCIAL ENTREPRENEURSHIP

Youth's desire to start both for-profit and not-for-profit ventures is probably a case of cognitive dissonance. This dissonance is a manifestation of the proclivity of youth to combine an entrepreneurial spirit with a philanthropic or social responsibility mindset. As with the basic dissonance generated by an intense desire to start a business without the knowledge of how to proceed, the dissonance created by the conflicting wishes to start both for-profit and not-for-profit ventures can be reduced in one of three ways. First, teenagers can choose to forgo permanently starting a not-for-profit venture to initiate a profit-making enterprise, or vice versa. Second, these young people could say to themselves that one or the other of these aspirations is of secondary importance and can wait until later. Third, high school students can pursue another dissonance-reducing strategy: they can introduce a new cognition. In this case, the new cognition involves combining the intrinsic goals of youth's two aspirations and providing them with access to knowledge about *social entrepreneurship* as a career alternative.

It is important that youth understand that in fact they do not have to choose between their two goals. The pursuit of social entrepreneurship represents a realistic alternative pathway for those students interested in reconciling both aspirations without necessarily becoming a prince or princess of darkness that uses unethical and illegal business practices, such as those that had been employed by Enron, WorldCom, or Global Crossings. In other words, for those entrepreneurship-oriented young people who are seeking a more immediate outlet for their philanthropic convictions, how might they pursue both objectives in parallel?

Social entrepreneurship could be a potentially exciting and viable option for these teenagers because it addresses concurrently their goals with respect to community philanthropy and entrepreneurship. As a relatively new phenomenon, social entrepreneurship entails mobilizing entrepreneurial resources and business practices to create and operate ventures that enact socially beneficial change. Social entrepreneurship further entails adopting social change goals as part of the missions and cultures of those ventures.

Overall, the non-profit sector in the United States is composed of 1.4 million non-profit organizations of diverse sizes and missions. It includes voluntary non-profit organizations and associations, public charities, and private foundations that are often created to improve the community by providing education, health, social, or other services, or by advocating for social or economic change. By some estimates the non-profit sector accounts for 5.2% of the GDP in the United States, and the sector has been growing more rapidly than other sectors in the economy.[7]

This size and growth makes the non-profit sector a fertile ground for social entrepreneurship, which has been on the rise in the United States. The leaders of these social enterprises have to act as entrepreneurs because they organize, manage, and assume the risk for an enterprise even if it operates as a non-profit rather than as a for-profit entity. In addition, preliminary evidence suggests that some proportion of new profit-making ventures that were organized over the last decade have been enterprises that seek to solve social problems or address community needs. These social entrepreneurs then deploy practices traditionally associated with business management and the entrepreneurial process to deliver their solutions.[8]

There are many examples of well-regarded and reportedly effective social enterprises that address important problems both in the United States and around the world. Such examples include: (1) Muhammad Yunus of the Bangladesh-based Grameen Bank who won the 2006 Nobel Peace Prize for pioneering the provision of microfinancing to poor men and women in developing countries;[9] (2) Jump$tart, which recruits and trains college students to work with low-income preschool children and their families to promote school success; (3) the Calvert Social Investment Foundation, which raises capital from private and institutional investors, lends it to socially oriented organizations, then returns it to investors, with interest; (4) Housing Works, which runs several retail establishments and a catering service to generate revenue that supports its housing, health and advocacy work for low-income, often homeless, HIV positive New Yorkers; and (5) Ashoka, which is a venture capital firm and global association of social entrepreneurs that provides owners of social enterprises fellowships, stipends, training, and access to a global network of peers.[10] For the owners and corporate cultures of all of these companies, giving back to society is also "good" business.

Developing young peoples' awareness of social entrepreneurship – and how their desire to contribute to their communities can be accomplished through entrepreneurial activity – should be an important part of any school curriculum that focuses on entrepreneurship. Such awareness would supplement youth intent and motivation with the knowledge necessary to actualize the connection between making positive social change and starting one's own enterprise. Encouraging social entrepreneurship awareness for our youth may contribute to income growth and prosperity for the country as a whole and for less advantaged groups in particular.[11]

There is another route to social entrepreneurship beside starting or leading a non-profit organization or starting a for-profit enterprise to help solve a social or community problem. This other route actually is the one that most major entrepreneurs take. They create enormous wealth in the for-profit sector and give a good portion of it away in the non-profit sector. In the words of Jon Huntsman, an entrepreneur and philanthropist who has donated millions to cancer research and shelters for battered women: "Too many wealthy people are under the mistaken impression that the true meaning of financial success ... is what you keep. It's ultimately how gracious you are and what you can do to make the world a better place."[12]

It may be the case that many high school students have thought about the path from for-profit entrepreneurship to major philanthropy and aspire to do both in that sense. These students are attracted to entrepreneurship because they have some knowledge already, and they believe it is the best vehicle for accumulating enough wealth to "really give back." They may believe they can do so through access to entrepreneurship and seek entrepreneurial role models with strong philanthropic track records.

Philanthropy is enjoying a new renaissance in the United States. From 1994 to 2004, the number of private foundations increased by 75% and the total giving by foundations rose from $11.3 billion to $31.8 billion.[13] More than 80% of all funding for charity comes from the public and major donors who themselves or their families were entrepreneurs. These contributions are aimed at finding solutions to high-value problems that seek to improve society in such areas as poverty, education, health, and literacy. The list of top individuals who donated or pledged to donate at least one billion dollars or more to charity in the 2002–2006 period included Warren Buffett ($40.6 billion), Bill and Melinda Gates ($3.4 billion), George Soros ($2.1 billion), Gordon and Betty Moore ($2.1 billion), Herbert and Marion Sandler ($1.4 billion), Eli and Edythe Broad ($1.4 billion), and the Walton Family ($1.1 billion).[14]

It is not surprising that so many of our young people yearn to be part of this golden era of giving. Many educators already are addressing effectively issues related to social entrepreneurship, but the educational system has an opportunity to do so much more simply by choosing to provide young people with entrepreneurship education. Such an education needs to make connections to social entrepreneurship and give special emphasis to successful not-for-profit organizations. In this way, students can learn how the principles of entrepreneurship and entrepreneurial thinking are applied in the context of pursuing philanthropy, community improvement, and social change. In particular, students should study how decisions are being made by the new "venture philanthropists" who are using to great advantage the basic business tools used by for-profit entrepreneurs.

Finally some extrapolations are in order to get a sense of the magnitude of the interest in giving back. These extrapolations are similar to those reported in the previous section except now they focus on social entrepreneurship. Over six in ten (64%) high school students said in their survey interviews that they wanted to start non-profit or charitable organizations to help their communities. Nothing is known about how likely these youth are to pursue these aspirations because that question was not asked. If, however, their likelihood of interest in social entrepreneurship is about the same as that of for-profit entrepreneurship (54% very likely or likely), then it can be estimated about one-third of all high school students (or 35,000 of every 100,000 students) are expressing a strong preference for participating in social entrepreneurship. This potential pool of social entrepreneurs can become a major source for innovation and community improvement. If a larger number of youth could be shown the connection between entrepreneurship, both for-profit and non-profit, and learned more about the main source of philanthropy, then those youth who received such education may have a greater desire to put their entrepreneurial knowledge and skills to work in helping society when they become adults.

KNOWLEDGE AND CURRICULUM

Currently in the United States, the high school academic curriculum is oriented toward preparing young people to join the wage economy – to take a job rather than make a job. High school students, in the best circumstances, acquire literacy, language and presentation skills, basic mathematics useful in many workplaces, and a general understanding of science that is designed to familiarize them with the scientific method and enable them to evaluate scientific claims.

What high school students rarely receive is any instruction in their schools on how businesses or non-profit organizations operate, and the knowledge, skills, or habits of mind necessary to practice entrepreneurship, either in the for-profit or non-profit arena. Given these conditions in the schools and circumstances for students, it should not be a surprise to find from the test items administered to students that most youth lack the knowledge of a select set of basic concepts and ideas related to entrepreneurship or about economics and, in addition, do not feel confident in their ability to use their knowledge and skills to start businesses.

Of course, such a short test as was administered to high school students and the discussion of those results does not fully present or describe the knowledge, skills, or habits of mind that should be taught in a quality curriculum that focuses on preparing youth for entrepreneurship, for-profit or non-profit, and an understanding of the world of economics in which that entrepreneurship will occur. To complete this discussion there needs to be a further extrapolation or explanation of the key concepts and connections that should be part of a high-quality curriculum for entrepreneurship.

It is easier to conceptualize this curriculum for entrepreneurship as a pyramid with three layers that progressively build toward an understanding of entrepreneurship, entrepreneurial thinking, and economics. At the base is a "Foundation" layer that addresses fundamental literacy and problem-solving skills necessary for the higher-level learning and doing that is required for participation in the entrepreneurial economy. In the middle is a "Bridging" layer that develops basic knowledge and skills in business management and essential communications – oral, written, and the use of technology. At the top is the "Focus" layer that emphasizes the practical skills people need to start a business, and covers the understanding of economic concepts of importance to entrepreneurs.[15]

This book essentially focuses on the entrepreneurship and economics content contained in the upper layer of the curriculum pyramid because that is what is needed for practical entrepreneurship.[16] What follows is a short description of five of the major components of the knowledge and skills people need to start a business. It is followed by a description of five of the economic concepts of key importance to entrepreneurs because to become entrepreneurial in their thinking and be entrepreneurs, youth must understand the connection between entrepreneurship and the underlying mechanisms of a market economy. It is these two essential components of a high school education that will help potential entrepreneurs to be successful and effective, and also help all students become entrepreneurial in their thinking and actions regardless of their livelihood or interests.

Entrepreneurship Component

1. A key component of entrepreneurship is *opportunity recognition*. In an economic environment characterized by rapid changes in technology, information, demographics, and global competition, it is critical for youth to see the opportunities for creative initiative behind the trends and within the gaps of their environment. Young people need to frame problems as opportunities, rather than as undesirable crises. Too often, problem solving is presented as a negative proposition rather than a positive experience that can expand possibilities. Entrepreneurial thinkers focus on the possibilities of each challenge rather than on its burdens. It is also important to base an entrepreneurial venture on an idea or opportunity that targets a realistic market niche capable of supporting the venture over time.[17] It is not sufficient simply to recognize opportunities; a good idea does not represent necessarily an entrepreneurial market opportunity.

2. Well-constructed blueprints help entrepreneurial ventures or functions succeed in their niche markets. These *business plans* must test well for

reality and define a compelling "value proposition" for their target customers or users – value based on actual benefits customers perceive they will derive from the features of the proposed service or good.

The plans also should reflect an ongoing commitment to the quality of production and the delivery of services or products to the complete satisfaction of their users.   The knowledge and skills required for effectiveness in these areas include being able to read (or listen to) and to analyze critically entrepreneurial venture plans or business plans.   These capabilities also presume an understanding of what is needed in such plans to chart the course of the proposed ventures and to provide an acceptable basis for assessing their prospects for success.

The writing of a business plan helps entrepreneurs think through the needs and requirements for starting a venture.   Some aspiring entrepreneurs get halfway through its writing only to realize their business idea is not realistic or feasible.   Other aspiring entrepreneurs increase their enthusiasm for starting a venture after writing a plan, because they see how their dream can become reality.   Additional reasons for writing a plan include the fact that it helps provide the documentation often required to obtain funding.   A well-constructed plan can also serve as a guide – a kind of "road map" for the business.

3. Learning to marshal key *resources*, especially start-up capital and an initial team of talented associates, is one of the most challenging hurdles for initiating any kind of entrepreneurial function or venture.   For the most part, these are resources over which one has neither direct ownership nor authority, at least at the outset.

Furthermore, these resources must be located and their commitment somehow secured for a proposition whose success cannot be guaranteed. This element drives an important knowledge requirement: young people must understand "what it takes" to start a business.   This includes the spectrum of tangible resources (money, space, supplies...) and intangible resources (time, labor, expertise, quality control...) needed to start and operate a venture.   Understanding is maximized if young people learn where such resources are most likely to be found, and discover the options for committing them to uncertain propositions whose objectives carry risk.

4. Resources must be tracked and managed, and one basic skill used to accomplish this task is *accounting* and record-keeping.   Learning how to make the best use of these tools allows people to monitor the employment of resources so they can be effectively used for the growth of the business. Accounting is critical for measuring how a new venture is doing.

5. Entrepreneurial ventures are not successful unless they have a team with an extraordinary ability to master *selling and pricing* of their product for

their target customers and users.   This team must be able to persuade potential customers to exchange something of value, such as money or time, for products or functions.   Advertising and selling are knowledge and skill areas individuals need to draw on as they try to convey a passion for the goods and services of the business (or for a non-profit initiative).

The degree to which their advertising and promotion skills translate into successful selling is also a function of young people's understanding of how to price products for their target markets. Entrepreneurs must be able to price their products taking into account such factors as market demand, competitors' pricing, production and operating costs, and desired profit margin. They also must construct effective messages that communicate the benefits of the product relative to its price.

Economics Component

1. One of the fundamental precepts of economics is that any time a decision is made there is an *opportunity cost*. In making a decision, a person gives up the opportunity to select the next best alternative. What was given up is considered the measure of the real cost of that decision.

Entrepreneurs continually make decisions as they adjust their businesses to meet market variations, such as changes in consumer demand, costs, or competition. For each decision, they must evaluate whether the benefits are greater than the opportunity cost. Youth can learn how to recognize this cost and factor it into their decision-making.   In doing so, they will better appreciate the relevance of economic reasoning to successful decision-making for an entrepreneurial venture.

2. Prices are determined in competitive markets through the interaction of *supply and demand*. Suppliers try to sell their products to consumers at the price that maximizes their profits.   Consumers, wanting to maximize the value of their money, tend to buy less at higher prices. It is the interaction of the conflicting perspectives of buyers and sellers that establishes the market price for a product and how much of that product will be sold.

Understanding how markets work often is a mystery to those uneducated in basic economics. As a result, people may complain about the outcomes from a market because they view a resulting price as either too high or too low. In some cases, government intervention is sought to mitigate the effects of market outcomes without a full understanding of the broader economic consequences of such interventions. Such a lack of awareness may result in policies that hinder entrepreneurship.

3. At the federal, state, and local levels, *government* plays a major role in a market economy. Its many activities include collecting taxes; spending

funds on public programs; regulating commerce; providing a court system which helps enforce contracts; and supporting measurement standards. These functions can be beneficial or harmful to business formation and operation, depending on context.

The entrepreneur needs to understand what government can do for good or ill to affect business operations. The enforceability of contracts is a key requirement for successful venture initiation growth. Many businesses also rely on the government's stabilization of measurement standards. On the other hand, the way certain taxes are levied can change the way a business operates. Some business regulations may tend to stifle entrepreneurship and raise the cost of doing business. Attempts to control prices historically have often led to market shortages.

4. High *inflation* results in a serious distortion of the value of money. This distortion makes decision-making more difficult because it is hard to calculate the costs and benefits of an economic decision. It also tends to erode the value of assets. This problem is especially challenging for entrepreneurs. They need to know how to take the inflation factor into account in such activities as selling products, purchasing resources, and managing the operation of their businesses.

5. In today's global economy, youth must understand the skills and knowledge areas that will enable them to compete in an *international economy*. The modern venture is operating in a world with increasingly fewer boundaries, a trend that demands unflagging and timely attention to the rapid oscillations of foreign and domestic markets. The changes in these markets affect many considerations, such as competition, pricing, resources, employment, and innovation. Such changes also represent both expanded opportunities and heightened risk for businesses.

The above set of core knowledge and skills about entrepreneurship and the basic concepts for understanding the functioning of a market economy should give high school students the basis for starting a venture, whether it is designed as a for-profit or not-for-profit venture. They are the two main components of an entrepreneurship curriculum for youth. If more youth had been taught such knowledge and skills in the schools, then more would be prepared and confident to start such new ventures at some point in their lives.

MARKETS AND MINDSETS

Knowing that high school students are embedded in a social environment that fails to provide them with a context for entrepreneurial thinking, it should not be surprising to find that students would harbor opinions about government and markets that were inconsistent with the attitudes of business owners and, therefore, with their own entrepreneurial aspirations. The survey results showed, for example, that about the same proportion of teenagers aspired to start their own ventures as they believed that businesses should be prohibited from raising prices when there is an increase in consumer demand. Few business owners would support price controls that would inhibit their ability to adjust to changing demand, so the fact that high school students did support price controls in this case indicated an area in which their development of an ownership mindset is far from complete.

The inconsistent attitudes of young people regarding their own potential entrepreneurship on the one hand and government control of markets, regulation and taxation on the other, is at least partially attributable to the fact that many high school students find themselves in a social environment that does nothing to help them develop identities as *producers* or owners, and to understand the forces of supply and demand. The social and educational environment in which young people are raised and educated affects their opinions and attitudes toward a variety of subjects including their political beliefs and their views toward the appropriate functions of government. Young people get their ideas from the mass media, their family, their community, their friends, and their schools.[18] The consumer-oriented mindset of teenagers is fed and nurtured in a culture outside of school. High school students are prepared, by default, to define themselves as consumers. This outcome occurs not because they are taught overtly to be consumers in schools, but because today's mass media and the heavy advertising targeted at the teenagers encourages consumption. In general, schools do little or nothing to counter this consumer orientation. High school students also are clearly consumers outside of school because they spend most or all of their disposable income on consumer goods, and they also highly influence the spending of their families for many other goods and services. As such, they exert a certain market power: businesses that cater to the tastes of teenagers are rewarded in the marketplace.

It is also difficult to develop a producer or ownership mindset within schools because they are structured as government-run institutions. In the marketplace, consumers have two options for action when confronted with a consumption choice. First, they can *exit*, which means they can choose not to purchase a product, or if they stay in the market, they may switch to another provider. Second, consumers can opt to use their *voice* to complain about a product or service that is unsatisfactory. In either case, their degree of *loyalty* toward the organization providing the product influences whether they decide to "vote with their voice," or "vote with their feet."[19] The most interesting aspect of this two-tiered consumer power is that the second option depends on the first: complaints carry weight if exit is a viable threat. If a company risks losing customers, it has an incentive to respond to consumer voice.

If they are unsatisfied with the quality of their public education, however, high school students, as users of educational services, generally cannot choose to exit. For most, short of becoming "drop-outs," they do not have the choice to opt out of school altogether because typically they are minors and switching to other providers of educational services is often not a realistic option. When alternative schooling is available, it often presents significant disincentives in the form of cost and of ancillary burdens on both student and parent. Usually, parents and students also only have a weak voice of influence in shaping the organization because there are other stakeholders with more power who determine the direction of this government-run institution. Students therefore lack consumer leverage when demanding better educational service, and they never consider producers or suppliers of educational services as responding to their demand as they would see in the marketplace.

What can be concluded from the school experience for most teenagers is that there is little in its organizational structure or in the education that is provided that helps students develop their knowledge and skills, or their entrepreneurial thinking. Young people learn about the world of business, entrepreneurship, and economics in the socialized system of schooling, and as a consequence they have little opportunity to learn, or much less appreciate, what it takes to be a producer or owner in society rather than just a consumer. It is understandable given these conditions that many teenagers develop an anti-business attitude and think that government offers the solution to change or problems, and therefore should do more to protect consumers from price increases, regulate markets, and tax businesses. Teenagers are educated and lead their social lives in an environment in which public policies determine almost every aspect of activity, from their class schedule, to the curriculum offered, to the system of reward. Outside schools, where people must participate in the economy either as employees or employers in order to attain economic well-being, markets, as well as government policies, play a part in determining what activities are rewarded.

Whereas support for price controls, more regulation, and higher taxation may be justified in light of high school students' in-school and out-of-school surroundings, these views also prevent young people from accurately evaluating government actions regarding the market in the light of their own potential for small business ownership and economic advancement in the future. When elected representatives or voters choose to raise business taxes, require licensing fees, enforce codes and conditions, or set price limits, they may be placing a burden on businesses. Whether such actions are justified is a matter of serious public debate. The acceptance of government intervention also depends on the care taken by government officials to establish regulatory regimes and incentive structures that seek to advance a particular social goal and at the same time do the least harm to businesses. It is important that teenagers perceive and comprehend these trade-offs and legitimate debates that often arise from government intervention in private markets and business decisions. Many young people who are interested in potentially starting their own businesses lack this ability to see the trade-offs or understand the complexity of the debates because they do not get such a perspective in school and see the world only from the eyes of a consumer. Some teenagers, however, are more fortunate to have access to adult entrepreneurs as family members or mentors, and therefore have the opportunity to acquire entrepreneurial knowledge outside of school, thus gaining a better appreciation of how markets work and the effects of government intervention.

MORE EDUCATION AND MORE OPPORTUNITY

The skills, experience, knowledge, and habits of mind necessary for successful entrepreneurship and entrepreneurial activity are often left out of the academic high school curriculum, and also typically are distinct from the curriculum offered in vocational or business programs in U.S. high schools. These vocational or business programs often have been offered as an alternative to the academic or college-preparatory curricula and have been designed for those students who might choose not to pursue postsecondary education. As such, these programs are intended to train wage earners and skilled workers to take trade, crafts, manufacturing, or office jobs, rather than to prepare young people to make their own jobs by becoming business owners. The difference between vocational or business education as it has been traditionally organized in high schools and what is advocated here is fundamental. Preparing young people to control their means of production and future livelihood, no matter what their background, history, or aspirations, requires them to have a sound understanding of entrepreneurship, business, and economics.

The challenge for the schools is to figure out new ways to provide such a quality education in entrepreneurship for high school students. Offering a dynamic course in entrepreneurship is only one step in the process, but there is much more that needs to be done to prepare youth to think in entrepreneurial terms and to start for-profit or not-for-profit ventures. School administrators, teachers, and parents and guardians need to see the vital connection between the lifelong knowledge and skills learned from an education in entrepreneurship and recognize the increased potential for long-term contributions during adulthood from such an education, not only for making a living or accumulating wealth, but also for the community and society in terms of a more productive economy, increased employment, and greater philanthropy. The effort also goes beyond schools and includes community groups and business organizations that have a vital stake in promoting entrepreneurial thinking and entrepreneurship.

The multiple benefits of an entrepreneurship education accrue both to the individual, and certainly to society and communities. Schools and community leaders all have a role to play in developing entrepreneurial knowledge and skills in high school students. In addition, more national, state, and local leaders who are concerned with improving education in the schools need to express their views publicly and take actions to promote entrepreneurship education.

Educational reform that introduces instruction in entrepreneurial skills would be an important development. A quality education in entrepreneurship would not only teach skills of opportunity recognition and business planning, it would also introduce these students to the many resources that are available for anyone who wants to start a business. Many organizations help small businesses owned by young people to organize their production, raise capital and find ways to reach customers.

Entrepreneurship education also can help young people to recognize their own strengths and expertise grounded in their community and family experiences. All young people have their own "funds of knowledge" derived from what they know about the people around them and what those people need. Most young people who become entrepreneurs take advantage of their lack of financial commitments to launch low-cost ventures, often out of their homes or dorm rooms. The growth of online commerce, combined with the comfort that many young people have with computers and the Internet, has introduced new opportunities for enterprising young people with minimal access to financial capital.

A quality education in entrepreneurship would introduce students to the importance of maintaining good relationships with a network of people who can provide useful resources for mentors. Not only do many young people lack financial backing for their ventures, they often also lack social capital, which not only entails the emotional support of family members, teachers, and community members, but also includes access to resources embedded in social relations. Understanding and pursuing the entrepreneurial process helps youth both to realize the importance of and to develop a network of contacts that provides useful information about business opportunities in the first place and also provides access to people – whether they are partners, expert consultants and professionals, skilled employees, or customers. Fortunately for aspiring young entrepreneurs, the technology and communications in the economy offer many opportunities for socializing and making connections. What is lacking is not young people's desire to start their own ventures, nor is there a short supply of financial resources, markets or customers. Instead, young people have not been prepared to reach for their dreams.

The initiative to advance entrepreneurship education offers a particular benefit to students from low-income communities for whom entrepreneurship often is the optimal strategy for economic and social mobility. One of the great purposes of schools in the United States is to provide, for all young people in the country, an "alternative inheritance." Many teenagers from low-income families, minority or immigrant communities, and residents of inner-city neighborhoods or rural areas have limited access to income-generating opportunities that could improve their socioeconomic position and move them into higher income brackets. For many of these high school students, entrepreneurship is the best option for economic advancement when they become adults.

Finally, it is important to restate, amidst all this talk of launching ventures and business ownership, that even for those young people who do not start their own ventures, having entrepreneurial skills is important. Of course, not all youth are born with a desire to start a business, nor is business ownership necessarily the best choice for every young person. Career aspirations among the young can vary substantially and are more likely to focus on jobs in medicine, law, engineering, sciences, or the arts. What often is missing from career preparation in the schools is the realization that entrepreneurial knowledge and skills are essential to the success of many careers even if the person never starts a business. A select group of people who are already suited to become entrepreneurs would therefore not be the only ones to profit from educational reform that introduces entrepreneurship instruction to the schools; future artists, scientists, doctors, lawyers, politicians, and people in all types of work also would benefit.

NOTES

1. www.sba.gov/advo/press/06-04.html
2. For examples of works on how economists view the relationship between entrepreneurship and the economy, and how it has been studied, see

Schumpeter (1934), Schramm (2006), Acs and Armington (2006), and Audretsch (2006).

3. For the results described in this paragraph, see Bruce, Deskins, Hill, and Rork (2007).

4. Phelps (2007) discusses the importance of the entrepreneurial culture to economic growth in the United States compared with Europe. Audretsch and Keilbach (2004) use the term entrepreneurship capital to describe cultural, institutional, and historical influences on economic performance. Schramm (2006) describes the importance for the United States to stimulate and support this entrepreneurial culture within all types of organizations.

5. These data on entrepreneurial activity are from Fairlie (2006).

6. See discussion related to Table 2.4 and Kourilsky and Walstad (2002).

7. Data on the non-profit sector are reported by the National Center for Charitable Statistics at the Urban Institute and in its annual *Nonprofit Almanac*.

8. See Cordes, Steuerle, and Twomby (2004) for an exploratory analysis of the extent of social or non-profit entrepreneurship in the U.S. economy. For a discussion of how to make social entrepreneurship work, see Dees, Emerson, and Economy (2002).

9. Greene (2006).

10. For a discussion of award-winning social enterprises (#2–5 in this paragraph), see Garcia, Lesova, Swindler, and Tuggle (2006).

11. See Delgado (2004).

12. Greengard (2006).

13. The number of foundations increased from 33,807 in 1994 to 67,763 in 2004, the latest year for reporting. These data, statistics on giving, and other facts about foundations are reported by the Foundation Center (www.foundationcenter.org).

14. See Woolley and Leak (2006).

15. For a complete description of the origins, interpretations, and content of this curriculum, see Kourilsky and Walstad (2000), Chapters 5 and 6. The contents of this curriculum underwent extensive review, study, and validation by many entrepreneurs, economists, educators, and leaders of several organizations concerned with entrepreneurship education for youth.

16. For the sake of brevity, the description of the many knowledge and skills in the foundation and bridging layers are omitted here and can be found in Kourilsky and Walstad (2000), Chapter 6. This following description of the focus layer is an abbreviated version of this work.

17. The terms "market" and "customers" are used to suggest not only the more traditional interpretation related to potential purchasers of goods or services in a market economy but also to include the broader interpretation of potential "customers" or "users" of any forms of goods

or functional services, including those that may be provided internally by an operating unit of an existing organizational framework, such as a communications group, an integration testing and quality assurance department, a research and evaluation unit, or a floating office assistant pool.

18. Csikszentmihalyi and Schneider (2000).

19. Hirschman (1981) defined the three responses: exit, voice, and loyalty for members of organizations, including employees, and members of states (citizens) who were confronted with failure in these organizations or states. Chubb and Moe (1988) discussed related concepts as they pertained to educational organizations.

References

Acs, Z., and C. Armington (2004), 'Employment growth and entrepreneurial activity in cities', *Regional Studies*, **38** (8), 911–927.

Acs, Z., and C. Armington (2006), *Entrepreneurship, Geography, and American Economic Growth*, New York: Cambridge University Press.

Acs, Z.J., and D.B. Audretsch (1988), 'Innovation in large and small firms: An empirical analysis', *American Economic Review*, **78** (4), 678–690.

Acs, Z.J., and R.J. Phillips (2002), 'Entrepreneurship and philanthropy in American capitalism', *Small Business Economics*, **19**, 189–204.

Audretsch, D.B. (2006), *Entrepreneurship, Innovation and Economic Growth*, Cheltenham, UK and Northampton, MA, USA: Edward Elgar.

Audretsch, D.B., and M. Keilbach (2004), 'Entrepreneurship capital and economic performance', *Regional Studies*, **38** (8), 949–959.

Baumol, W.J. (2005), 'Small firms: Why market-driven innovation can't get along without them', *The Small Business Economy: A Report to the President*, Washington, DC: Office of Advocacy, U.S. Small Business Administration, 183–207.

Bednarzik, R.W. (2000), 'The role of entrepreneurship in U.S. and European job growth', *Monthly Labor Review*, **123** (7), 3–16.

Benavot, A. (1983), 'The rise and decline of vocational education', *Sociology of Education*, **56** (April), 63–76.

Bernanke, B.S. (2007), 'The Level and Distribution of Economic Well-being', Speech at Washington, DC Federal Reserve Board, February 6.

Beroff, A., and T.R. Adams (2000), *How to be a Teenage Millionaire*, Irvine, CA: Entrepreneur Press.

Birch, D.L. (1987), *Job creation in America: How Our Smallest Companies Put Most People to Work*, The New York Free Press.

Boykin, A.W., R.J. Jagers, C.M. Ellison, and A. Albury (1997), 'Communalism: Conceptualization and measurement of an Afrocultural social orientation', *Journal of Black Studies*, **27** (3), 409–418.

Braunstein, S., and C. Welch (2002), 'Financial literacy: An overview of practice, research, and policy', *Federal Reserve Bulletin*, November, 445–457.

Bruce, D., J.A. Deskins, B.C. Hill, and J.C. Rork (2007), *Small Business and State Growth: An Econometric Investigation*, Washington, DC: Office of

Advocacy, U.S. Small Business Administration (under contract SBAHQ 05 M 04100).

Burt, R.S. (1992), *Structural Holes: The Social Structure of Competition*, Cambridge, MA: Harvard University Press.

Carree, M., and A.R. Thurik (2006), *Entrepreneurship and Economic Growth*, Cheltenham, UK and Northampton, MA, USA: Edward Elgar.

Chubb, J.E., and T.M. Moe (1988), 'Politics, markets, and the organization of schools', *American Political Science Review*, **82** (4), 1065–1087.

Cordes, J.J., C.E. Steuerle, and E. Twomby (2004), 'Dimensions of nonprofit entrepreneurship: An exploratory study', in D. Holtz-Eakin and H.S. Rosen (eds), *Public Policy and the Economics of Entrepreneurship*, Cambridge, MA: MIT Press, 115–151.

Council of Economic Advisors (2000), *Philanthropy in the American Economy*, Washington, DC: Council of Economic Advisors.

Csikszentmihalyi, M., and B. Schneider (2000), *Becoming Adult: How Teenagers Prepare for the World of Work* (1st ed.), New York: Basic Books.

Davis, S.J., J.S. Haltiwanger, and S. Schuh (1996), 'Small business and job creation: Dissecting the myth and reasssessing facts', *Small Business Economics*, **8** (4), 297–315.

Dees, J.G., J. Emerson, and P. Economy (2002), *Strategic Tools for Social Entrepreneurs: Enhancing the Performance of our Enterprising Nonprofit*, New York: John Wiley.

Delgado, M. (2004), *Social Youth Entrepreneurship: The Potential for Youth and Community Transformation*, Westport, CT: Praeger.

Eckel, C.C., and P.J. Grossman (1998), 'Are women less selfish than men? Evidence from dictator experiments', *The Economic Journal*, **108** (448), 726–735.

Ericksen, G.K. (1997), *What's Luck Got to Do With It? 12 Entrepreneurs Reveal The Secrets Behind Their Success*, New York: John Wiley.

Fairlie, R.W. (2004), 'Does business ownership prove a source of upward mobility for blacks and Hispanics?', in D. Holtz-Eakin and H.S. Rosen (eds), *Public Policy and the Economics of Entrepreneurship*, Cambridge, MA: The MIT Press, 153–179.

Fairlie, R.W. (2006), *Kauffman Index of Entrepreneurial Activity: National Report, 1996–2005*, Kansas City, MO: Ewing Marion Kauffman Foundation.

Festinger, L. (1957), *A Theory of Cognitive Dissonance*, Evanston, IL: Row, Peterson.

Garcia, T., P. Lesova, J. Swindler, and K. Tuggle (2006), 'Class of '07: The Fast Company/Monitory Group Social Capitalist Award winners', *Fast Company*, **111** (December), 70.

Giving USA Foundation (2005), *Giving USA 2005: The Annual Report on Philanthropy for the Year 2004*, Indianapolis, IN: Center of Philanthropy at Indiana University.

Greene, J. (2006), 'Taking tiny loans to the next level', *Business Week* (November 27), 76–80.

Greengard, S. (2006), 'Money for nothing', *American Way* (September 1).

Haltiwanger, J., and C. Krizan (1999), 'Small business and job creation in the United States: The role of new and young businesses', in Z.J. Acs (ed), *Are Small Firms Important?: Their Role and Impact*, Boston: Kluwer Academic Publishers.

Hirschman, A.O. (1981), *Exit, Voice, and Loyalty: Responses to Decline in Firms, Organizations, and States*, Cambridge, MA: Harvard University Press.

Kantor, J.S. (2006), *I Said Yes! Real Life Stories of Students, Teachers and Leaders Saying Yes! to Youth Entrepreneurship*, Ashburn, VA: Gazelles, Inc.

Kaplan, A.E., and M.J. Hayes (1993), 'What we know about women as donors', *New Directions for Philanthropic Fundraising*, **2**, 5–20.

Karlsson, C., C. Friis, and T. Paulsson (2006), 'Relating entrepreneurship to economic growth', in B. Johansson, C. Karlsson and R.R. Stough (eds), *The Emerging Digital Economy: Entrepreneurship, Clusters and Policy*, Berlin: Springer-Verlag.

Katz, M.B. (1989), *Reconstructing American Education*, Cambridge, MA: Harvard University Press.

Kent, C. (1990), *Entrepreneurship Education: Current Developments, Future Directions*, New York: Quorum Books.

Kiyosaki, R.T., and S.L. Lechter (1997), *Rich Dad, Poor Dad*, Scottsdale, AZ: TechPress.

Kourilsky, M.L. (1999), *Making a Job: Guide to Entrepreneurship Readiness*, Kansas City, MO: Ewing Marion Kauffman Foundation.

Kourilsky, M.L., C. Allen, A. Bocage, and G. Waters (1995), *The New Youth Entrepreneur*, Camden, NJ: Education, Training, and Enterprise Center (EDTEC).

Kourilsky, M.L., and W.B. Walstad (2000), *The "E" Generation: Prepared for the Entrepreneurial Economy?*, Dubuque, IA: Kendall/Hunt Publishing.

Kourilsky, M.L., and W.B. Walstad (2002), 'The early environment and schooling experiences of high-technology entrepreneurs: Insights for entrepreneurship education', *International Journal of Entrepreneurship Education*, **1** (1), 87–106.

Kourilsky, M.L., and W.B. Walstad (2005), *The New Female Entrepreneur: Creating and Sharing the Wealth*, Dubuque, IA: Kendall/Hunt Publishing.

Kuratko, D.F., and R. Hodgetts (1998), *Entrepreneurship: A Contemporary Approach* (4th ed.), Ft. Worth, TX: Dryden Press.

Lambing, P., and C. Kuehl (1997), *Entrepreneurship*, Upper Saddle River, NJ: Prentice Hall.

Levesque, K., D. Lauen, et al. (2000), *Vocational Education in the United States: Toward the Year 2000*, NCES 2000–29, Washington, DC: U.S. Department of Education, National Center for Educational Statistics.

Lowrey, Y. (2006), 'Women in business', *The Small Business Economy: A Report to the President*, Washington, DC: Office of Advocacy, U.S. Small Business Administration, 55–91.

McGrath, R.G., and I. MacMillan (2000), *The Entrepreneurial Mindset: Strategies for Continuously Creating Opportunity in an Age of Uncertainty*, Boston, MA: Havard Business School Press.

Minniti, M., I.E. Allen, and N. Langowitz (2005), *Global Entrepreneurship Monitor 2005 Report on Women and Entrepreneurship*, Kansas City: Ewing Marion Kauffman Foundation.

National Council on Economic Education (NCEE) (2005), *Survey of the States: Economic and Personal Finance Education in Our Nation's Schools in 2004*, New York: NCEE.

Orman, S. (2001), *The Road to Wealth: A Comprehensive Guide to Your Money*, New York: Riverhead Books.

Phelps, E. (2007), 'Entrepreneurial culture', *Wall Street Journal* (February 12), A15.

Pryor, J., et al. (2006), *The American Freshman: National Norms for Fall 2006*, Los Angeles, CA: Higher Education Research Institute: University of California, Los Angeles (www.gseis.ucla.edu/heri/norms06.php).

Rooney, P.M., D.J. Mesch, et al. (2005), 'The effects of race, gender, and survey methodologies on giving in the US', *Economics Letters*, **86** (2), 173–180.

Schramm, C.J. (2006), *The Entrepreneurial Imperative*, New York: HarperCollins.

Schumpeter, J.A. (1934), *The Theory of Economic Development*, Cambridge, MA: Harvard University Press.

Severens, C.A., and A.J. Kays (1999), *1999 Directory of U.S. Microenterprise Programs*, Washington, DC: Aspen Institute.

Stanley, T.J., and W.D. Danko (1996), *The Millionaire Next Door: The Surprising Secrets of America's Wealthy*, Atlanta, GA: Longstreet Press.

Swartz, J. (2006), *Young Wealth: Trade Secrets from Teens Who are Changing American Business*, Bloomington, IN: RoofTop.

Taylor, M.A., and S. Shaw-Hardy (Eds.) (2006), *The Transformative Power of Women's Philanthropy*, New Directions for Philanthropic Fund Raising, No. 50, San Francisco: Jossey-Bass.

U.S. Census Bureau (2006), *2002 Survey of Business Owners* (SBO) (www.census.gov/csd/sbo/).

U.S. Census Bureau (2005), *Statistics for Industry Groups and Industries: 2004 Annual Survey of Manufacturers*, Washington, DC: Economic and Statistics Administration (www.census.gov/prod/2005pubs/am0431gs1.pdf).

U.S. Census Bureau (February 2002), *Voting and Registration in the Election of November 2000. Current Population Report*, Washington, DC: Economic and Statistics Administration (www.census.gov/prod/2002pubs/p20-542.pdf).

U.S. Department of Agriculture (2004), *2002 Census of Agriculture*, **Vol. 1** (Geographic Area Series Part 51), Washington, DC: National Agricultural Statistics Service (www.nass.usda.gov/census/census02/volume1/us/USVolume104.pdf).

U.S. Department of Labor, Bureau of Labor Statistics (2005), *Volunteering in the United States, 2005*, Washington, DC: United States Department of Labor.

U.S. Small Business Administration, Office of Advocacy (December 2006), *The Small Business Economy: A Report to the President* (www.sba.gov/advo/research/sb_econ2006.pdf).

Walstad, W.B. (1992), 'Economics instruction in high schools', *Journal of Economic Literature*, **30** (December), 2019–2051.

Walstad, W.B. (1994), *Entrepreneurship and Small Business in the United States: A Gallup Survey Report on the Views of High School Students, the General Public, and Small Business Owners and Managers*, Lincoln, NE: Ewing Marion Kaufmann Foundation, Kansas City, MO, Center for Entrepreneurial Leadership.

Walstad, W.B. (2001), 'Economic education in U.S. high schools', *Journal of Economic Perspective*, **15** (3), 195–210.

Walstad, W.B., and Kourilsky, M.L. (1996), 'The findings from a national survey of entrepreneurship and small business', *Journal of Private Enterprise*, **11** (2), 21–32.

Walstad, W.B., and M. L. Kourilsky (1998), 'Entrepreneurial attitudes and knowledge of black youth', *Entrepreneurship Theory and Practice*, **23** (2), 5–18.

Walstad, W.B., and M.L. Kourilsky (1999), *Seeds for Success: Entrepreneurship and Youth*, Dubuque, Iowa: Kendall/Hunt Publishing.

Walstad, W.B., and K. Rebeck (2000), 'The status of economics in the high school curriculum', *Journal of Economic Education*, **31** (1), 95–101.

Walstad, W.B., and K. Rebeck (2001), 'Assessing the economic understanding of U.S. high school students', *American Economic Review: Papers and Proceedings*, **91** (2), 452–455.

Wennekers, S., and R. Thurik (1999), 'Linking entrepreneurship and economic growth', *Small Business Economics*, **13**, 27–55.

Woolley, S., and Leak, B. (2006), 'The top givers', *Business Week* (November 27), 72–75.

Zinth, K. (February 2007), 'Entrepreneurial education laws in the states', *State Notes: Economic/Workforce Development*, Denver, CO: Education Commission of the States.

Index